(CONTINUED FROM BACK COVER)

on the town, brought her breakfast each morning, walked her dogs (who slept at the foot of his bed), and carried messages between Margaret and the Queen mother, who sometimes didn't speak to each other for days.

Payne was on hand to witness the Queen's disappointment at her younger sister's choice of a fiancé, and to help Tony accustom himself to the unfamiliar formalities of Clarence House, and he won the young photographer's affection by rescuing him from awkward breaches of royal protocol.

Here is the exclusive, surprising, and intimate account of a royal servant who sometimes served his Princess vodka with her orange juice, who tells whose picture was on her bedside table when she said "Yes" to Tony, who knew her private feelings about public appearances—and who loved his Princess because of her whimsies and despite her foibles.

My Life

with

GOLD MEDAL BOOKS

Princess
Margaret

by David John Payne

An Original Gold Medal Biography

Fawcett Publications, Inc., Greenwich, Conn.
Member of American Book Publishers Council, Inc.

Chapter One

In the distance, the gradual swell of cheering from the crowds and the faint jumbled clip-clop of horses' hooves announced that the beautiful Princess would soon come into sight, near the end of her long drive to Westminster Abbey.

And I waited, among the thousands who stood under the clouds of that dull May day, to see her, Princess Margaret, on her way to her marriage to a commoner, former photographer Antony Armstrong-Jones. The marriage had been a surprise; there had been hitches—like the blazing publicity over the choice of best man, who later begged off—and there had been misgivings.

But now on the day itself the people turned out, everything else forgotten, to cheer, to wave, to shout and to pay their tribute to the lovely young woman who long ago had won the hearts of Britain and the rest of the world. They had come from all over the face of the earth, these people who lined the route along the famous Mall, Birdcage Walk, Whitehall and Parliament Square and—where I was—outside the majestic Abbey itself.

Many had stayed up all night, sitting on the curbs, camping in the green open spaces of St. James's Park, many of them bivouacked with their national flags flying proudly over their heads. . . . Australia, Canada, New Zealand, U.S.A., Sweden, Germany. They, and millions more who saw it on television then and later, watched, drawn by the fascination of seeing again the Princess they had heard and seen often enough, but did not really know. But I knew.

I had been close to Princess Margaret for months, going with her where she went, attending to her, seeing and talking to her every day, observing the real person behind the

Royal mask. The real person who was both Her Royal Highness, the Princess Margaret—and Margaret, my Princess.

And now I had come to see her once again, to stand and watch, and to make my own personal wish for her future happiness.

The cheering grew louder, nearer now . . . but my mind slipped back to those days only a few months before, when I shared the everyday secrets of her personal life in her service as her personal footman.

I knew her mind; I knew her moods. I had seen my Princess happy and sad, bubbling with excitement and in a storm of Royal fury. I had seen her heart, broken by her last goodby to her first love, Peter Townsend, mend under the stimulus of her last love, Antony Armstrong-Jones—the man she was coming to marry this day.

As I stood, jostled by the crowd whose excitement was growing by the minute, I remembered the time Peter Townsend came to tea at Clarence House, and how I had been with him, Margaret, and the Queen Mother when they made their last farewells. And how, later, the Princess threw aside Royal protocol and abandoned herself to a whirl of nightlife in London's West End clubs and theatres with a constant variety of escorts.

I remembered the runaway weekends she shared with her future husband, Tony. How they went off to Royal Lodge, Windsor, to spend carefree and romantic hours dancing until the dawn, and those midnight meetings at the swimming pool in the spacious gardens of the Lodge. I was the only witness, the only person who could see clearly, even in those early days, that Margaret was falling in love with this man from the "outside." This other so-called commoner.

I smiled to myself, there in the crowd, at the jokes I had shared with Margaret, the way she had teased me, the small delightful little incidents which were always cropping up to make life with my Princess so unforgettable.

And all the other thoughts came crowding in. . . . The time I got a "rocket" from the Queen; the time Margaret was "stood up" for a dinner date by Tony Armstrong-Jones. Those embarrassing times when Tony asked me to cash checks for him because he was due to take Margaret out. . . . The time Margaret and another escort came home with the morning papers. . . . The way she "cheated" with the money I gave her for the church collection plate.

The "Crankpots" and the unknown admirer who became her favorite; the quarrel she had with Tony, and the time she perplexed the Royal gardeners by cutting a big ragged hole in one of their precious hedges. The evenings that she and Tony spent together in the private cinema at Clarence House—and the other evenings they cooked for themselves at Tony's Pimlico flat-*cum*-studio.

And of the man she was now minutes away from marrying. . . . The time Prince Philip lost his temper with Tony and swore; how the Princess's suitor hid in his bedroom when the Queen stopped in for a drink at Royal Lodge. . . .

The people around me were shouting now. "There it is, can you see?" they asked each other. I looked over and saw the top of the magnificent carriage with its escort of Household Cavalry.

And I thought back to the times I had seen Margaret washing her pet dogs, and of the thousand other things I knew about her—that she did not drink champagne, paid for her own dresses, did her own hair, applied her own make-up.

I saw Margaret dressed in sloppy sweater and slacks, almost prim in a severe afternoon dress, beautiful in an evening gown, ready for a ball. . . . And the night she and the Queen Mother led the whole lot of them in a crazy Conga line up and down the stairs of Clarence House.

I watched as the carriage drew closer and caught a glimpse of the tiny figure in white waving gracefully to the crowd and looking adorable and serene.

It was a bit different when those of us in Margaret's little party had spent a night in a crazy Scottish castle with candles and barely a fire in the place.

Now my thoughts were banished by the noise, the cheering, the clatter of the hooves, and the laughing chatter of those around me. Margaret stepped from her coach, trailing yards of train behind her gorgeous wedding dress, and walked, almost gliding, into the Abbey, out of which she would return with a new life ahead of her.

How is it that I, the humble son of a country bricklayer, came to know so much of Margaret's old life?

I will tell you.

Chapter Two

It was while I was in service at the St. James's Palace home of the press proprietor, Lord Rothermere, that I heard, through the servants' grapevine, that a vacancy had cropped up in the Royal Household at Clarence House. They were looking for a footman.

Immediately I wrote to the Comptroller at Clarence House, Lord Adam Gordon, and asked if it were possible that I might be considered for the position. In my letter, I set out my experience as a footman to Lord Rothermere and of my former services as an officer's steward in the Royal Marines.

To my delight and surprise, I received a letter from the Comptroller by return post. I thought it would be no more than a note saying that my application had been received, or something like that. But no. On official Clarence House notepaper, Lord Adam had written asking me to come for an interview with him the following day.

All that night, I rehearsed my "speech" to Lord Adam, meaning to impress him with my bearing and control of the situation. But when the day dawned, the butterflies in my stomach would not be stilled. Hours before it was necessary, I dressed myself in my best suit, a dark gray double-breasted affair, and carefully knotted my gray tie around a shining white collar. It was a fine day, so I wore no coat or hat.

I walked along to the main gate of Clarence House and rang the bell of the police lodge, which is situated just inside the gates.

In response to my ring, the door was opened by a uniformed policeman who looked at me with that natural suspicion that comes so easily to policemen. I cleared my throat and told him my name was Payne and I had come to keep an appointment with Lord Adam Gordon. At this, his brow relaxed.

"Yes sir, we are expecting you," he admitted.

I waited while he went back to his lodge and picked up a telephone. He dialed a number and spoke. I heard snatches of conversation . . . "He's here now, sir . . . I'll have him brought up right away. . . ."

He told me to wait for someone to come and collect me and eyed me up and down as if measuring a prospective ally. I stood there for perhaps five minutes until I noticed a Queen's Page coming toward me. I admired his smart uniform, navy blue with gold epaulets on the shoulder and the Royal crest in gold on the left breast pocket of his battle-dress tunic. And I remember wondering if I, too, was destined to wear a similar uniform.

The page came up to me and asked: "Are you Mr. Payne?" I nodded, and he motioned me to follow him across the concrete courtyard and down a flight of stone steps at the corner of the House, to the left of the main front door. Together, we plunged into the gloom of a long stone-flagged corridor on which our footsteps echoed like drums. I went along blindly for a moment or two, before my eyes got accustomed to the gloom.

We twisted and turned in a seemingly endless trail of winding passages beneath Clarence House until finally we came to the foot of a rickety wooden staircase. The Page bounded up the stairs lightly and confidently, but I did not share his confidence in the strength of the stairs, and I walked up gingerly, resting my hand on the splintered wooden handrail.

At the top of the stairs, the world changed. I was surprised to find I was back again at floor level, and through an elegant doorway I entered a thickly carpeted hallway—more the sort of setting, I thought, which you would expect in Clarence House.

Along this corridor, which I later discovered led to the rear entrance to the House, we passed doors leading into the offices occupied by the officials connected with Her Majesty, Queen Mother, and Princess Margaret. At the far end of the hall was a narrow doorway. The page stopped

outside and motioned me to wait. Then he knocked on the
door and, without waiting for a reply, entered.

I heard him address someone inside the room. "Here
is Payne, my Lord," he said. Then he stepped from the
doorway and motioned to me to enter the room.

I walked into the room and was struck by the apple-
green paintwork; it seemed to relax me, somehow. But I
had little time to examine my feelings, for on entering the
room, Lord Adam Gordon—for it was he—stood up behind the mahogany desk at which he had been sitting. I
took stock of him. He was about five feet four in height, rather
dapper, with graying hair and a slim, neat build. He was
dressed conservatively in a dark gray lounge suit, a white
shirt with a stiff collar and a silver-gray tie. But the most
startling thing about him was the pair of thick, horn-rimmed
glasses which gave him an air of authority.

Almost without thinking, I glanced around the room. . . .
I took in the desk, littered with papers and the two armchairs, one on either side of the desk.

Once in the room, I closed the door behind me, and as
I did so, Lord Adam quickly removed his glasses, and I
felt his eyes flicker over me, searching for his first impressions of me. He came round the desk and held out his
hand. He smiled and said: "Please sit down, Payne." He motioned me to one of the leather armchairs by the desk.
I sat down, and for a moment or two he left me to my
own thoughts while he rummaged thoughtfully through some
of the scattered papers on his desktop. He picked up and
dropped half a dozen sheets of paper before he found
what he wanted—the letter I had written him a couple of
days before. I racked my brain trying to remember what
was in it.

After a quick scan of my letter, Lord Adam started
questioning me about my previous experience in domestic
service.

He asked: "What experience have you had waiting on
table and valeting? Both these, of course, will be quite essential if you enter service in the Royal Household." I
told him that these duties had been part of my service at
St. James's Palace, and he nodded as if satisfied. There followed one of those inevitable pauses, always a little embarrassing, which are likely to crop up during any interview, so I

launched into an account of my service with the Marines and my past life in general. He listened attentively, and interjected a few more questions.

Finally, as if reaching a decision, he said: "Of course, I shall have to take up a reference from Lord Rothermere's secretary...." I felt my heart leap. Surely, I reasoned, if he went that far, the job would be mine. I felt it would now be a question of going back to St. James's and awaiting his next call. But his next words brought me back to earth with a jolt.

"You will be seeing Her Royal Highness this afternoon. Will you be free to stay to lunch?"

I nodded, speechless. This afternoon! I most certainly had not prepared myself to be received by the Princess, and the prospect rather unnerved me. But Lord Adam was talking again: "I don't think there is much doubt that you will be accepted as personal footman to Her Royal Highness," he said. "You are tall, smart, and seem to have the bearing required to carry out your duties."

I was overwhelmed by this, all the more so because of the almost offhand manner in which Lord Adam told me that one of my wildest dreams had come true.

Lord Adam then gave me a little coaching for my first meeting with Princess Margaret.

"You will address her always as Her Royal Highness," he said. "Speak up when you answer her, and don't be nervous."

He said the last words with some emphasis. I suppose because it must have been obvious that I was already nervous.

Then he brought up the subject of what I would be paid in Royal service—something which I had not thought about since I first applied.

"You will be paid a basic wage of five pounds ten shillings a week. From this, of course, income tax and National Insurance will be deducted."

This was the same pay exactly as I had been getting in Lord Rothermere's service, so I already knew that in fact the pay I would actually draw after these deductions would be four pounds eleven shillings a week.

Altogether, my interview with the Comptroller lasted about half an hour. Before we parted, he stood up and asked: "You will stay to lunch then?" I said I would, thank you, and he reached over his desk and pressed a small button. Instantly, there was a knock at the door, and the same Queen's Page entered. At this, Lord Adam turned to me, held out his hand again and said: "Thank you very much, Payne. I wish you good luck, and I do hope you will be happy working here in the House."

I thanked him, and he told me, finally, that confirmation or otherwise of my appointment would be telephoned to Rothermere House within a day or two. At that, I turned and left the room with the page, who was waiting to take me straight to lunch with the other servants in the servants' hall in the basement.

Outside the door, the page rather brusquely strode away, leaving me to follow him. He paced rapidly and familiarly, with me striding uncertainly behind him. We retraced our steps down the rickety wooden stairs, past the steaming kitchens in the basement, and into the rather chilly, damp-feeling servants' hall. It was large and low-slung, stretching about twenty feet by fourteen feet wide. Like practically every corner of Clarence House, it was painted from floor to ceiling in cream. The floor was plain wooden planking, and spread in the middle of the room was an ordinary red and blue carpet.

On it stood the table at which we all ate. It was a large wooden rectangular thing with wooden-backed chairs placed all around it. The room was as stark as it could be. On one side was a large sideboard and on the other a hotplate used for keeping our food reasonably warm after it had been brought from the kitchen.

I tried to put my later appointment out of my mind and managed to work up quite an appetite. I was pleased to note that the table before me had already been laid for lunch. By this time, the other servants in the House who were not actually on duty with the Queen Mother and the Princess had gathered in the room and were waiting for their meal to be served to them by three young liveried attendants. Servants' servants, they were. At meal times, anyway.

My silent friend, the page, introduced me rather wood-enly to the rest of the staff, about twenty in all, and then he showed me to my place at the table. I hesitated, following everyone else as one does at these times. I wondered idly if someone would say Grace before the meal, but no one did. I sat down and my lunch was brought to me. It was already on the plate, rather to my surprise.

I must say that the lunch that day was like nothing I had anticipated or would have expected in the Royal Household. I didn't expect the best silver and caviar, but this. . . . I looked down at my plain white china plate, my appetite diminishing every moment. I glanced around a bit furtively, to see if the others would comment on it. But no, they fell to like hungry men. I shrugged, picked up my knife and fork and tackled my meal. It was a small portion of grilled liver, mashed potatoes and runner beans, the whole liberally sprinkled with thin gravy.

I did not know it then, as I chewed on the rubbery liver, that throughout my service at Clarence House, the meals for the staff would not improve, either in the cooking or the grinding choice of menu.

But as the meal progressed, I became increasingly conscious of the interview I was to have somewhere upstairs which might decide my future—and food became less and less important. In fact, I was not sorry that conversation at lunch was not easily forthcoming from the other servants.

The only other thought which intruded throughout lunch was that the place in which I was eating could have used some good, old-fashioned Royal Marine chow.

Lunch lasted about forty minutes in all, and I had barely time to light a cigarette before my page approached me and asked if I would go with him to meet Mr. Kemp.

Jack Kemp, as I discovered shortly, was Steward to the Household. He had been in the Queen Mother's service for some forty years, throughout her reign as Queen and later when as Queen Mother she retired to Clarence House with Margaret. He was the man responsible to Lord Adam Gordon for controlling the male staff at Clarence House. It was his job to look after the wine cellars, the liveries of the servants, traveling arrangements for any of the staff who went away with either the Princess or the Queen Mother. In fact, anything which had to do with the internal running of the household.

I was to come into contact with Jack Kemp almost every day of my service, and he was usually to be found in his neat little office adjoining the pantry on the ground

floor. Mr. Kemp was one of the most pleasant persons I
ever met, and I got on with him very well from the first
moment I met him. We chatted in his office for about
forty-five minutes, and he spoke as if I had already got
the job. He told me something about my duties, and we
talked about the Princess herself. It was obvious from the
first that he was very fond of Her Royal Highness, and he
had the habit of referring to her as the "little lady." Then
he said, "I suppose we shall have to call her *your* little
lady now, John." Mr. Kemp looked at his watch—it was
shortly before 2:30 p.m.—and he told me it was time to go
along to see the Princess herself. I swallowed hard . . . and
followed him into the main corridor which ran from the
front door of the house right up to the grand main staircase.

On fawn carpeting, richly laid throughout, we walked
under the constantly burning chandeliers—they were always
lit because the corridor was so dim. Mr. Kemp led the
way along this corridor toward the front door. When we
were about ten yards from it, he turned abruptly left.

I followed, and found myself in a narrower corridor,
at the far end of which, facing us, was the door to Princess Margaret's sitting room. But before we go through the
door and on with the story, let me give some idea of what
this constantly used main corridor was like. This was the
passage through which everyone who was anyone in Royal
circles walked, from the Queen herself, down to . . . well,
applicants for jobs, like me.

During the short walk with Mr. Kemp, I had noticed a
number of large oil paintings hanging on the walls in the
main corridor—all of them ancestors of the Royal families
and of the Queen Mother. One large canvas particularly
caught my eye. It was a full-length portrait of the late King
George VI, husband to the Queen Mother, who died in 1953.
It was framed in ornate gilt and hung on the right-hand side,
as I walked towards the main door. Above the portrait there
was an electric light which spotlighted the rich colors, the
reds, blues, purples and golds of the robes of the Order of the
Garter which had been worn by the late King at the time of
the portrait. It was a truly majestic picture and the most eye-
catching of the lot.

And it was later to be the witness to one of the most poignant moments of all my months in Clarence House.

However, to my mind, the rest of the corridor seemed overcrowded, cluttered in fact, with pieces of furniture. Two long settees upholstered in gold colored brocade stood on either side of the corridor, beside two large glass-fronted cabinets which contained china dinner-services—hundreds of years old and worth thousands of pounds. These were illuminated with small lights inside the cabinets. Scattered everywhere, or so it seemed, were little round occasional tables. Actually, there were six of them, three on each side, two of them bearing big vases of flowers in white porcelain stands.

As we proceeded toward Margaret's sitting room the corridor along which Mr. Kemp and I walked was even dimmer than the one before. It was lit by lamps bracketed to the wall on both sides, but as the right hand side was largely walled by bookcases—they were filled with books, which as far as I know were never touched—the effect was to plunge the corridor into patches of shadow.

I passed another settee on my left, similar to those in the main corridor, and two backbreaking Chippendale upright chairs. We passed one door on the right which led to the Lancaster Room, into which I was to show dozens of visitors. However, at this moment the scenery was a misty blur.

I was so nervous I nearly collided with Mr. Kemp when he stopped suddenly outside the white-painted door to Margaret's room. He turned to me, and his face creased in a friendly smile of reassurance. He nodded briefly, then rapped on the door with the back of his hand. I automatically straightened my tie, silently cleared my throat, and wished fervently that the butterflies in my stomach would fly away.

From within the room a small high-pitched voice called: "Come in."

Mr. Kemp opened the door—and I was in the presence of my Princess for the very first time.

The door swung open, and my attention was immediately riveted on Margaret, a tiny figure, beautiful in a pink and white cotton dress, her dark hair brushed into a bouffant style and a shining double row of pearls round her throat. I stood, exhilarated by the exquisite perfume Margaret wore as Mr. Kemp said in his well-modulated tones: "Your Royal Highness, this is Payne. He has come for his interview."

I walked into the room and as I did so Margaret rose from her chair with a rustle of petticoats. She walked to meet me with a restrained but friendly smile on her face. She extended her small white hand—I had time to see the smoothness of the skin and the care which had gone into the manicure of her nails—and we shook hands. Her grasp was warm and firm, not at all the limp hand I had half-expected from her.

With easy charm she said, "Good afternoon, Payne. Do take a seat." She indicated one of the large armchairs placed on one side of the fireplace. I waited while she settled herself in a similar seat on the other side of the fireplace. She sat perfectly self-possessed. A yard from her I sat as nervous as a child.

I had seen Princess Margaret before on a number of occasions, but only at a distance. She had been little more than a smiling face through a car window or one of a crowd of important people. I remembered, too, the glimpse I had caught of her once when she was exercising her three dogs in St. James's Park. It had been about a year ago. And one other time, six years earlier when I had been part of a Royal Marine ceremonial guard outside Westminster Abbey on the day Margaret's sister Elizabeth had been crowned Queen of England.

These memories flashed through my mind as Margaret sat an arm's-length from me, a lovely figure, cool and completely at ease. I studied her face, the face hundreds and hundreds of newspaper and magazine photographs had not done justice.

Margaret, at twenty-nine was a beautiful woman.

Her face, not too heavily powdered, had been made up by an expert—herself, as it later turned out. Her eyebrows had been penciled in and her lipstick smoothly formed in delightful cupid's bow. But her most striking, almost mesmeric features were her enormous deep blue eyes which now flashed a friendly smile across to me as she began the most important interview of my life.

Smoothing the full-skirted dress over her nylon-clad knees she began quite simply.

"Now, Payne, I want you to tell me all about your previous appointment. Who were you with last?"

I said: "I was a footman to Lord Rothermere." And then I added hastily, "Your Royal Highness."

Margaret nodded. "Yes. And how long were you with him?"

"One year, Your Royal Highness." It struck me as being a bit of a conversation-stopper to keep saying 'Your Royal Highness' but I remembered the words of Mr. Kemp and continued to call her that. So the conversation between the lovely princess and myself went on.

"Tell me, what did you do while in his employment?"

"Waiting on tables, Your Royal Highness, and valeting and cleaning the silver."

Margaret nodded again thoughtfully. She had been smoking throughout our conversation, using a long cigarette holder which I judged to be made of gold. Now she leaned forward, uncrossing her legs as she did so, and demurely flicked the ash from her cigarette into a gleaming silver ashtray on a small table at her side.

"I'm told you were in the Royal Marines, is that right?"

I guess she had grown tired of learning about my experience with Lord Rothermere's silver, and I too was glad of a change of subject.

"Yes, Your Royal Highness," I answered. "I was in the service for . . . let me see, six years in all."

She leaned back in the armchair, more interested now. She wanted to know where I had been with the Marines. I told her that I had been as far as Canada and America and had spent some time in the West Indies Station.

This struck an immediate response from her and her eyebrows raised.

"Oh," she said. "As your probably know, I have been to the West Indies, too, and I enjoyed myself there very much indeed." She was referring, I knew, to her fabulous tour of the West Indies in 1955 when she took the islands by storm and left behind her the echo of a hundred calypsos dedicated to her by the delighted inhabitants. She asked me if I knew Jamaica well. As it happened, I did.

"I once spent two weeks leave on the island, Your Royal Highness, and I don't know any more lovely spot in the world."

As we talked about those far-off islands in the sun I felt my nervousness slip from me, melted by the warmth of her personality. We talked on for a few minutes more before she said, "I'm sure you know, and Lord Adam Gordon will have explained, what your duties will be here." Suppressing my excitement, I told her that it had been outlined to me.

At this Margaret rose suddenly and decisively. She lay down her now empty cigarette holder and once again proffered her hand.

"Well, Payne, I do hope you will be happy while you are working with me."

In my excitement I stumbled out a few words of thanks, bowed slightly, backed away from her a pace or two and turned towards the door.

I was stopped halfway by Margaret inquiring: "Oh, one moment, what are your Christian names?"

"David John," I said, puzzled.

"And what are you normally called?"

"I . . . er . . . I prefer to be called John, your Royal Highness."

"Very well," said Margaret brightly. "John it will be."

I opened the door and walked out of the room, having heard that my wildest ambition was all but fulfilled. I, the humble son of a country bricklayer, was to be the personal servant of the Royal Princess whom the whole world adored. No wonder I was walking on air.

I left the Princess standing in the room in which she spent the greater part of her day in Clarence House. Within a few weeks, I was to become familiar with every item in it. It was a pleasant apartment decorated in a shade of pale green with a white ceiling, and a light gray pile carpet on the floor. In front of the fireplace, which had been boarded up and fitted with an electric heater, lay two Persian rugs, one pale pink, the other blue. It did not seem to me the kind of decor that Margaret herself would have chosen. But it must be remembered that Margaret could not have any say in the decoration of Clarence House, for it is, after all, the Queen Mother's home, and at that time the Princess was only sharing it with her.

Nevertheless, the sitting room had a pleasant enough aspect. Across the room from the door were two windows through which one could see the garden, the Mall, and, further on, the green expanse of St. James's Park. The left-hand window, a full-length one, gave access onto a small stone-paved terrace where Margaret liked to walk in the sunshine. Both windows were draped down to the floor in white net and heavy, pale pink satin curtains.

Between the windows was Princess Margaret's desk and a bow-legged Chippendale chair with a green and white striped seat. On the desk itself lay a leatherbound blotter and a silver ink stand with inkwells for red and black ink in which stood two long pens.

Margaret often wrote at this desk. She always liked to answer her personal mail in her own hand and every day she religiously wrote in her personal diary with one of the half-dozen fountain pens which she kept in a little silver tray on her desk. At either end of the desk, quite typically, stood a leatherbound frame with pictures which Margaret herself had taken while on holiday with the family in Scotland. To the left, she kept the shot of the Queen Mother dressed in a tartan skirt and tweed jacket, sitting on the grass in front of Balmoral Castle; the right-hand frame contained two pictures, one each of Princess Anne and Prince Charles.

Directly in front of Margaret as she sat at this desk was a crucifix—a simple cross fashioned in oak with the figure of Christ carved in ivory. It was about six inches high.

In the far left-hand corner of the sitting room, near the French window, stood a small table, constantly groaning beneath the weight of dozens of the latest British, American and Continental magazines; adjacent to this table were the familiar settee and two chairs to match, all three covered with pink fabric.

Just inside the room and to the left, was a small table with a bust of the Princess carved in marble, about two feet, six inches high. I think Margaret was quite fond of the little carving, but I was never able to think of it as anything but a chunk of stone, for no sculpture, no painting could ever capture the spark of vivacity and alertness which characterized my Princess. The blank, staring eyes of the marble bust were a negation of what the Princess really was.

To the right and behind the door was the object which was, in many respects, the centerpiece of the room. It was

Margaret's stereophonic record player, of which she was justifiably proud. It was a fine instrument which reproduced music with the original full rich tones. Margaret loved to use it, playing any of the hundreds of records she kept in an adjoining cabinet, their gay covers making a rainbow of color along the shelves.

Next to the records, in the right-hand corner stood an eight-foot-high bookcase. Once again, the rows of tightly packed leatherbound books never appeared to leave the shelves. They were mainly history books covering a thousand years of turbulent English history—and Margaret's favorite reading was the latest popular novels, newspapers and magazines.

To complete this picture of Margaret's sitting room, there was the fireplace in the right-hand wall with two settees facing each other at right angles to the wall. At the end of each were the armchairs in which the Princess and I sat during the interview. Finally, dotted around the room were six or seven vases of flowers which it became my job to arrange each day.

This, then, was the room I left after my first introduction to Princess Margaret. My nervousness had vanished now, and I slowly became filled with a kind of exhilaration. In my bones, I knew I had made a good-enough impression on the Princess to get the job as her personal footman. And it was with an almost jaunty step that I walked back alone to the office of the Comptroller on the other side of Clarence house.

"How did you get on, Payne?" asked Lord Adam when I presented myself to him again.

"Very well, thank you, my Lord," I told him. "I feel sure the Princess was pleased with me, and I got the impression that she will accept me."

"Very well," he said. "When can you start?"

I told him that I thought it would be possible to take up the job the following Monday. That would be short notice for Lord Rothermere of course, but I felt certain that he would not stand in my way. I shook hands with Lord Adam and left the room, returning again to the pantry where I met Mr. Kemp. He shared my optimism, and he told me he would telephone me as soon as everything had been confirmed. With that, I left Clarence House by the back entrance and walked back again across the court to the Rothermere home.

My ordeal was over. I went through the whole thing in my mind and felt happy that I had performed well enough to get the job. And as I thought it over, I realized that in fact it had not been such an ordeal—thanks to the charm and warmth of my Princess.

The next two days could hardly go quickly enough for me. I found my concentration wandering again and again to the decision being made about me in the large, cream-painted building a hundred yards away.

Would my dream come true? . . . Were there other candidates for the job who were being told the same as I? . . . Would they have second thoughts about me?

These questions gnawed at my brain day and night.

Chapter Three

I did not have long to wait for my answers, though my nails were bitten to the quick by that time.

I took the call on the telephone in the Rothermere pantry. Another of the staff had answered it and he handed me the black receiver with a nonchalant: "It's for you." I do not suppose he saw how my hand was shaking as I took it and said, with a husky voice: "Hello, this is Payne."

"Hello," said a voice at the other end. "This is Mr. Kemp speaking. Good morning." My stomach was playing me tricks and doing somersaults, but I tried my best to control myself and asked carefully: "What is the news?"

"You have nothing to worry about, old chap. You are in. You will be starting on Monday, if that is all right with you."

All right with me! I almost danced on the spot. I felt like running over to Clarence House at that very moment. I was in! I was to be a member of Princess Margaret's staff—the sort of job that a thousand normally unemotional butlers would have given their ears for.

But I hoped I sounded calm enough as I took a deep breath and said: "Thank you very much. I will be delighted. I'll move in, if I may, on Sunday evening." That would be perfectly all right, said Mr. Kemp, and he hung up. I stood there in the pantry for fully two minutes after I had replaced the telephone receiver. I felt that if I moved, I would wake up. It took me that long to realize that my dream was real, and had come true.

Twenty-four hours later, I was packed and ready to leave Lord Rothermere's house. I had stuffed my belongings into my two rather weary suitcases and sat smoking, forcing myself to be patient and wait until after lunch to move over to Clarence House. At last, I pulled on my coat, picked up the bags and walked out into the courtyard. Three minutes later, I walked through the servants' entrance to Clarence House and I had officially arrived.

I had the House almost to myself. The Princess and the Queen Mother had traveled to Royal Lodge, Windsor for the weekend and would not be back until Monday afternoon. Consequently, many of the servants had taken weekend leave, and the house was maintained by a skeleton staff. I walked unnoticed and unheralded into the pantry and dropped my bags on the floor. But, of course, they were expecting me, and one of the servant's attendants was waiting to take my bags and show me to my room.

He told me that my room was on the first floor at the back of the older part of the house, overlooking York House, the Duke of Gloucester's town residence. He picked up my bags and led me through the stone corridor, up the wooden stairs to my door, threw it open, placed my bags inside and withdrew without a word.

I walked in and stopped dead in my tracks. I looked round in amazement. I lit a cigarette and leaned back against the wall—and later found I had wiped a big white mark onto my coat. To sum up my first reaction to the room, I was utterly depressed. I was not expecting a Royal apartment, but this cubbyhole, with its whitewashed walls and ceilings, made me think immediately of a monk's cell!

How could I ever make this place my home? How could I ever make this a place to retreat to after my day's work? I tried to console myself that one could get used to anything in time, but this would take an age to get used to. The approach to the room was bad enough. To get to it, I had to come up a flight of eighteen narrow stairs with a sharp and rather awkward righthand turn about six steps up. The stairs were lit by a single bulb in the ceiling which burned constantly. To try to negotiate the stairs in the darkness would have been to invite a broken neck. Even so, the light was not brilliant, but just bright enough to show me how worn and threadbare was the dark brown carpet which covered the stairs. The walls of the staircase offered little relief. They were painted in the same dull cream which covered practically every corner of Clarence House.

The stairway led onto a small landing from which my

door opened on the right. The door was painted cream, of course, and the whole aspect of the stairs, the landing and my door never ceased to depress me, and although I loathe getting up in the morning, it was always a relief to leave that part of the House and move down into something a little brighter.

That first afternoon, I stood, feeling rather chilly and damp, for some five minutes looking glumly at my little part of the fine stately home of Her Majesty the Queen Mother and Her Royal Highness the Princess. This is what I saw:

The room measured about six feet by eight. Opposite the door on the far wall was the window. It was about two feet in height and was set into the wall at about chest-level. Against this same wall stood my bed. This too made me feel a little unhappy. I judged it to be about five feet, six inches long, and I stand six feet, one inch tall. I feared that even my bed, that last haven of comfort, would be too cramped for me. My fears were justified. Throughout my stay at Clarence House, I was never able to sleep stretched out without my feet hanging over the end of the bed. Countless times I would wake up in the night with frozen toes, and although I asked on several occasions if my bed could be changed, I was always told there was no other available. In the end, I had to make my bed so that the blankets hung well over the end, in the hope that this would keep my feet warm. But the result was that I would wake up with half my body uncovered. I planned and fought to wring a good night's sleep out of that bed, but I rarely won, I'm afraid.

On the right-hand wall of the room was another window of roughly the same size, and behind the door stood a chest with two small drawers and three large ones in it. I found out that it was on this chest that I had to do all my personal valeting. I pressed my suits and livery on it with a borrowed iron plugged into a socket on the floor.

Two steps from the door, against the left-hand wall, stood my wardrobe, an ancient dark-stained thing which I judged to be older than I. It did not stand properly on the uneven floor-boards and was propped up with a piece of folded cardboard wedged under one corner. For the floor itself, someone had chosen a particularly flimsy linoleum, laid wall to wall. Near the bed was a rectangle of threadbare carpet.

Further along from the wardrobe was the fireplace. This had long ago been boarded up and had been replaced by an electric heater. By the fireside stood the only chair in the room, with wooden arms and a backrest padded and covered in a dark brown material.

And that was that. And if this paints a pretty depressing picture of a room, then believe me, it looked it. But this was not the end. It was not long before I was to share my room with three rather tiresome guests, the Princess's dogs.

I was informed about my lodgers on my second day at Clarence House. Mr. Kemp, the steward, called me over while I was in the pantry and asked: "Have you seen your little lady's three dogs?"

"Yes, I have seen them running about the house." I frowned. "Why do you ask?"

"Well. . ." Mr. Kemp hesitated. "I'm sorry to say that as there are no kennels for them and your little lady will not have them in her bedroom at night, they will . . . er . . . well, they will have to share yours."

I could only say: "Well, I'm damned! I can hardly turn myself round in the room without having three dogs as well."

But there was nothing for it. A Royal order was a Royal order. I had to accommodate them. Thinking back, of course, they were really very amusing, but at the time I wondered how on earth we should all fit in.

I shrugged and went off to the basement where Mr. Kemp had told me the dogs' baskets were kept. I collected them and heaved them up to my room. I puzzled over the problem of arranging them so that I would not always fall over them, and eventually hit on the only possible solution. I put one in the corner of the room at the end of the bed, one by the headboard and the other, for want of any other place, underneath the bed. In time, I got used to having my three guests, but from that day on, I'm afraid my bedroom always smelled rather like a kennel, no matter how often I bathed the dogs. Actually, it was my job to bathe two of them—the Sealyhams Johnnie and Pippin. Bath day was always an hilarious occasion. I had to run practically all the way around Clarence House to catch them, and although the three of us carried out the bath operation with great gusto and a good deal of splashing, the moment I had finished, Johnnie and Pippin would scamper straight out into the garden and roll in the mud.

But the third dog got special treatment. He was a lively little brown and white King Charles spaniel named Roly. Roly was the Princess's favorite and she always bathed him herself. In fact, he washed in the Royal bathroom adjoining the Princess's bedroom.

Poor Roly. He never really appreciated this honor, and used to skulk away whenever he was wanted for his weekly beauty treatment. I had to pick him up and carry him under my arm into Her Royal Highness's bathroom, as he fought to free himself. The Princess, on the other hand, looked forward to this chore. She would be waiting in the bathroom, with a jug of perfumed shampoo standing on the side of the tub. She ran a few inches of lukewarm water into the bath. Then she would stand back and, after a playful tickle of Roly's long ears, say to me: "All right, John, pop him in." Once in the water, Roly quite enjoyed the whole thing. The Princess used to kneel down by the tub and start to scrub him vigorously with her nails until he was covered from head to tail in white soapsuds.

Her Royal Highness took the precaution of wearing a dainty little pinafore over her afternoon dress on this important occasion, but against the energetic and not always willing Roly, it was never enough protection. By the time the bath was over, Margaret would be thoroughly soaked. And when he scrambled onto the mat he shook his head madly, spraying the bathroom and the Princess with water. But she was very deft at catching him up in the big bath towel, and laughed and tickled him as she dried him.

Then came the part they both liked most. Margaret stood Roly on a towel in the corner of the bathroom while she trotted into the bedroom to get her electric hair-dryer. She plugged it into the socket, then sat cross-legged on the floor with the dog and played the warm air over his long fur while combing him with a thick-toothed comb and flicking his curls into place. Roly loved it, standing there preening while the Princess cooed: "Pretty Roly. There's a lovely dog, isn't he, John?"

Without doubt, this was one of the most charming of

all the dozens of off-guard moments during which I came to know the charm of my Princess. Her lovely face slightly flushed and completely wrapped up in this homey job, she looked completely beautiful.

My three charges were not the only dogs in Clarence House, by the way. Queen Elizabeth, the Queen Mother, had her own two corgis called Billy and Bee and; a miniature dachshund named Ricky. All the dogs traveled wherever Her Majesty and Her Royal Highness went, riding in style in the Rolls Royces and on the Royal Trains.

None of them ever wore collars. In fact, the Royal dogs are the only ones which are not obliged by the law to wear collars when outside the house. The six of them were always scampering all over Clarence House and it is still a matter of amazement to me that they were never stepped on. I myself narrowly missed tripping on them many, many times.

Ricky was the most troublesome of them all. He had a habit of jumping up at people when they approached him. I believe the Princess, for one, quite loathed him, for once or twice he committed the terrible sin of jumping up and laddering her nylons with his paws. And that would be enough to earn the dislike of any woman, particularly a woman as dress-conscious as my Princess. In the end, she could not bear to have Ricky near her, and waved him away with her hands.

I really did not have charge of them until bedtime. During the day they spent all day with the Princess and the Queen Mother. But at night, before I could turn in, I had to go round the house calling Johnnie, Pippin, and Roly in the corridors and occasionally fetching them out of the Princess's sitting room. Then we went for a last walk round the garden—a necessary but hazardous ritual, since they liked to scramble around the bushes, and I had to try to keep my eyes on all three at once lest they disappear. But as they got used to the routine, they came fairly readily with me up to bed.

And, as my day ended with the dogs, so it would begin. The dogs woke first, of course. Then their favorite habit was to cavort around the room as soon as it was light. Very often my day started with a cold nose thrust into my face, or gentle licks over my face from all three at once. Believe me, it is hard to ignore three dogs all eager to be up and about, even when it is only 5:30 in the morning. I used to wrap myself up in the bedclothes and pretend they were not there, but there was no getting away from them when they began to scratch at the carpet, indicating that they were in urgent need of a walk! Then, for my own comfort, I had to clamber out, dress, and hurry them down into the garden for their first exercise.

They were irritating, awkward, demanding, and spoiled, but I grew very fond of them. They were part of my life with Princess Margaret.

It was on my first day at Clarence House that the question of my uniform arose. Mr. Kemp told me that an appointment had been made for me to be measured for my blue battledress-type uniform.

Once again, another of my illusions was shattered. I had imagined that the fitting of a Royal Household servant would be a matter of meticulous measurement by a host of tailors taking hours to make sure that the suit fitted in every detail. But no; the whole operation was over in ten minutes. One tailor and a bored-looking assistant recorded the barest details of my structure in quite a casual manner. With a final sigh, the tailor murmured: "Ready in three days." And back to Clarence House I went. For the next three days, I wore my ordinary dark gray lounge suit and a black tie.

Sure enough, three days later, the suit did arrive. I felt quite excited that I would at last be able to wear the official uniform of the Royal Household staff, so I went immediately to my bedroom and opened the brown paper parcel. The suit was a little creased in the parcel and when I laid it out on my bed and looked at its two pieces of thick, rough blue serge, it did not appear too promising. Anyway, I put it on. It was not exactly Saville Row. The trousers were too large in the waist and sagged horribly in the seat. The tunic was not too bad, except that when I did up the little hooks around the collar, it was strangle-tight. So my first job was to go downstairs and borrow needle and thread, remove the hooks and eyes, and sew them on again in a more comfortable position. This done, I could at least breathe, and managed to make myself look presentable.

The worst aspect of the uniform was that in the summer it became unbearably hot. I sweated freely and found the high collar most irritating. Another snag was that the suit, being made of serge, tended to pick up endless dog hairs, fluff and dust. To keep myself looking smart, I had to press the trousers at least every other day.

Nevertheless, the tunic, with its gold epaulets on the shoulder and Royal cipher on the left breast did make me feel a part of the Royal Household. When I finally went downstairs wearing it, I felt a glow of pride. In fact, I felt rather special, but of course everyone else had on a similar suit and no one really noticed.

My service with the Princess really began the day after I arrived at Clarence House. As I have said, both she and the Queen Mother had been away for the weekend at Royal Lodge. They were due to return Monday afternoon and I would see and speak to my Princess for the second time— but now as her personal footman.

For the arrival of the Princess, I took up my station on the pillared porch at the front door of Clarence House. I had opened the double front doors in readiness, and I stood in the sunlight waiting to usher her into the house. Not unnaturally, I was rather nervous during the five minutes or so that I stood there rehearsing how I proposed to show her in. I kept staring at the main gate, looking for the Princess's black Rolls Royce with the famous registration number, PM 6840.

The car drove in through the gates at about 3 P.M. and rolled silently to a halt right in front of the door. I sprang forward and opened the rear nearside door. There was a scurry of fur around my feet as the three dogs tumbled out and dashed inside, then the Princess stepped gracefully from the car, still carrying the dog leads in her left hand. She wore an off-white full-length woolen coat with a colored scarf about her neck, and as she brushed past me, I caught a whiff of expensive perfume. A few paces from the car, she turned and, with a handsome smile, said: "Good afternoon, John. It is so nice to see you again."

I bowed my head gravely and spoke for the first time to my new employer. I said simply: "Good afternoon, Your Royal Highness." She nodded, turned and walked out of the sun into the front door and out of sight along the corridor leading to her sitting room. I slammed the car door and followed her.

I walked into the house to begin learning the routine of the work involved in being personal footman to Princess Margaret. I was to find that the job had a hundred little details, was full of fascination and, despite the late nights and the early mornings, utterly rewarding.

I found Princess Margaret a wonderful person to work for. As time went on, I was able to pierce the shell of Margaret's public image and appreciate the warmth, the charm, the gaiety of this lovely, lively young woman.

My days with her in Clarence House fell naturally into a kind of routine. I don't mean that they ever lacked diversion, but ... well, this is what a day in the life of Princess Margaret was like.

Naturally, life in Clarence House began long before Her Royal Highness rose. For me, as I have said, it began with the dogs. My first chore of the day was to take them all for a walk in the garden. The house was quiet at that hour and the rest of London was only just beginning to awaken. It was most pleasant to stroll in the garden with the scent of flowers in the air or the mist rolling across from St. James's Park across the Mall at the end of the garden. However, I could not afford to linger too long, and after I had rounded up the dogs, I shut them in the sitting room, nipped up to dress myself properly and set about my work. The next thing was the newspapers. I walked across the concrete drive outside the front door and over to the police lodge by the main gate where the newspaper boy left the Princess's papers. I took them back to the pantry, and after tucking them away where none of the other staff could pick them up, walked across the hall to the orderly room where one of the staff sorted the mail into bundles—for the Princess, the Queen Mother and the Household staff. I stopped for a chat, perhaps, with the two attendants who manned the orderly room, then took her Royal Highness's letters back to the pantry and laid them with the papers in readiness to go on her breakfast tray.

By this time, it was about 8:15 and I sat down with the other staff in the pantry to have my own breakfast.

A quarter of an hour later, I started supervising the preparation of Princess Margaret's breakfast tray. I covered an ordinary wooden tray with a clean white cloth, picked up the papers and the mail and went down into the basement and the kitchen. Then it was a matter of minutes for cook and me to prepare breakfast.

The Princess always took the same breakfast. It was as simple as it could be, consisting only of a plate of fresh fruit—bananas, grapes, an orange and perhaps a peach. She never ate anything but this, and more often than not she would not touch even this simple repast. But she did enjoy a cup of tea. In the pantry, I boiled a kettle and made her a pot of weak tea in a yellow and white china teapot. From the cupboard, I selected Margaret's cup, saucer and two plates to match and arranged them on the tray together with milk and sugar. By 9 o'clock it was all ready and I carried the tray from the pantry, turning left along the hall to the Royal elevator. This was strictly "out of bounds" to all other Royal servants and was normally used only by the Princess and the Queen Mother when going to their upstairs apartments. However, for breakfast and at other times when I had to take things up to Margaret's second-floor rooms, I was allowed to use it.

The elevator was a small one, made to accommodate only four people. In fact, it rarely had to accommodate more than one, but had to be of a reasonable size to allow the Royal mother and daughter to use it when coming down in some of their beautiful gowns with wide, flared skirts and hoops. It was fitted with a large mirror facing the door and I imagine that it very often reflected the Princess giving her hair a final pat or inspecting her lipstick before she arrived at the ground floor and went out on some big occasion. However, in the mornings, it only reflected me with the Princess's tray snatching a glance at the headlines in Her Royal Highness's papers. The lift had a push-button control panel on the left-hand side of the door. It was richly carpeted in a thick brown pile, with gilt paneled walls and a brightly polished brass handrail around three sides.

With the tray balanced in my left hand, I pressed the button marked "2" and waited while the elevator ascended silently past the first floor where the Queen Mother had her suite of rooms. On the second floor, the lift stopped, the doors slid open, and I stepped out into the corridor. This ran in both directions from the lift and was about fifty yards in length. To the right at the end of the corridor was the grand sweeping staircase leading down to the first floor.

Opposite the lift were two doors leading to the rooms occupied by the Queen Mother's and Princess Margaret's dresser, Mrs. Ruby Gordon.

Mrs. Gordon was a devoted servant and friend to the Princess. She was in her forties and had been in the service of the Royal Household for some twenty-three years. She had grown up with Margaret and had looked after her since the Princess was a little girl of about six. Their relationship was an intimate one and there were very few secrets between them. But more of that on later pages. At the moment, let me give a picture of the second floor.

Adjacent to the dresser's rooms were two high wardrobes where Mrs. Gordon kept the Princess's vast collection of dresses. Between the two wardrobes was the door leading to the Princess's bathroom—the door through which Roly the spaniel kept his appointment with the bath. Finally, at the end of the corridor was the door to Margaret's bedroom.

I walked along to this door. I did not enter at this time, but placed the breakfast tray on a low, four-wheeled trolley parked outside. This done, I walked back to Mrs. Gordon's room, tapped on the door and called out: "Good morning, Mrs. Gordon, breakfast is ready."

Mrs. Gordon would be awaiting my signal to start her day by waking the Princess. We both walked along to the bedroom and while I waited, Mrs. Gordon—without waiting to knock—threw open the door and wheeled the trolley in. Briskly, she drove it up to the right-hand side of the bed, left it, and went over to pull back the curtains. She moved around the room flicking the curtains back and then perhaps she would return to the trolley and rattle a teacup waiting for the Princess to wake up.

But if the Princess had an official engagement to fulfill and she had to be up and about, it was a different matter. Mrs. Gordon would walk in, park the tray and say quite loudly: "Come along, Margaret. It's time you were up." That would be enough to rouse the sleeping Princess. She was a light, healthy sleeper and in any case, unless she had had a late night the evening before, liked to be up fairly early. And when she was away at Royal Lodge, Windsor, there was nothing she enjoyed more than rising early for a ride around the Park on one of her horses.

While the Princess stirred herself, Mrs. Gordon busied

herself around the room picking up the dress that Margaret had worn the night before, together with her shoes, cigarette lighter and holder, and any other items scattered around the room. I waited in the corridor for about ten minutes or so, while this went on.

When Mrs. Gordon reappeared, she handed me the shoes, lighter, and holder and I left the second floor. Then it was back to the pantry where I kept a selection of brushes and dusters in a drawer with polishes and creams of various colors. The Princess's shoes were all handmade and did not have any size marking on them, but I guessed they would be about size five, so I did not take too long to clean them. But I had to do them thoroughly or the ever-watchful Mrs. Gordon would hand them back to me, pointing to a speck of mud or something like it on the heel and with a look of anguish, would reproach me for not bringing them up to the standard required of a Princess. The lighters and cigarette holders also had to be spotless. I cleaned them thoroughly with pipe cleaners and white methylated spirit, filled the lighters with petrol, and checked to see that they were in proper working order.

Having done this chore, my next duty was to sort out Margaret's mail. I took her personal mail to her sitting room and laid it on her desk for her to read, when she came down shortly before lunch. While in the room, I dusted round the desk, tables and mantlepiece, watered the flowers and generally tidied up. Usually, there was a drink tray, a heavy silver one, and one or two dirty glasses which had been used the night before.

By this time, it was about 10 o'clock. My duties for the next hour took me all over Clarence House. There were orders to collect for the Princess's travel arrangements, if she was going away for the weekend and instructions from the Princess to carry out. She got into the habit of leaving instructions for me in her sitting room, written on small notepaper engraved with her name. These meant I had to alert the chauffeurs or arrange for some item to be collected from a shop. Sometimes, I had to carry messages for her outside Clarence House, but I was usually finished by eleven.

At that time every morning without fail, I collected a glass jug of fresh orange juice from the kitchen and carried it on a silver tray to the sitting room. From then on, it was merely my duty to wait for Her Royal Highness to come down. By eleven, she usually rose and went to the bathroom adjoining the bedroom, where Mrs. Gordon had prepared her bath.

During the two hours between breakfast and bath, the Princess lay in bed listening to the radio and thoroughly reading the newspapers, which she invariably left scattered over the bed and on the floor. Still, she was a Princess, and Princesses are entitled to do that sort of thing. While she lay there reading and listening, she usually lit up her first two or three cigarettes of the day, stubbing them out an inch long in the ashtray at the bedside.

At about the time the Princess got up, I went up to her suite to deliver the clean shoes, the lighter and holder. Mrs. Gordon wheeled out the breakfast tray—as I have said, it was rarely disturbed except for the addition of an ashtray with newly-stubbed butts.

After I had been well inducted into the routine of Clarence House and my part in it, I became quite friendly with Mrs. Gordon, normally a rather sharp lady who did not hesitate to put upstarts, like myself, well in their places. Not that she did it maliciously, for this was her way of protecting Margaret from anything approaching sloppiness on the part of the staff. There was no doubt that Mrs. Gordon was extremely proud and jealous of her very special position in the Royal Household, a position I became fully able to appreciate.

Chapter Four

During twenty-three years of service at Buckingham Palace and later at Clarence House, mostly with the Princess, Ruby Gordon had become very much more than a servant. This was especially true at the time I met them both, when Margaret had grown into a lovely young woman. Now the mistress-servant relationship played a minor role in the interchanges between the two women. Even their personalities had grown similar. Furthermore, being roughly the same size, they very often dressed in the same style. In this respect, Mrs. Gordon was fortunate, for Margaret would sometimes hand over a dress or an exquisite suit which she had worn only once or twice.

But the most revealing was the way they addressed each other by their Christian names. Mrs. Gordon is the only Royal servant who called Her Royal Highness "Margaret".

Often, when I went upstairs with the Princess's things, they would be carrying on a loud conversation from the bathroom to the bedroom. From the bath, Margaret might shout: "Ruby, you've forgotten my bath salts." Or: "Ruby, what dress are you putting out for me today?"

Once I was there when the Princess squealed from the bath: "Ruby, Ruby, I've got soap in my eyes," and Mrs. Gordon dropped what she was doing and hurried into the bathroom to help out.

In this and other ways, Mrs. Gordon would sometimes tend to treat my Princess as if she were still a little girl, with rather sharp commands to "Come along," or "Hurry up." But I suppose it was just the habit of half a lifetime, and I know that the Princess held Mrs. Gordon in very high regard indeed.

In some respects, Margaret depended entirely on Mrs. Gordon's taste. Often, her dress for the morning would be chosen quite arbitrarily by her dresser. She had a very large selection to choose from, of course, and each morning, unless the Princess asked specifically for a particular dress, Mrs. Gordon went to one of the twin wardrobes in the passageway and spent a few minutes ruffling through them to make up her mind. Occasionally, she would hold one of the dresses up to her and take a thoughtful look in the mirror. But once she had chosen, she picked out shoes to match and took them into the Royal bedroom and laid them out on the bed.

Only very rarely would the Princess crinkle up her nose and ask for something else. Her first dress of the day was usually a cotton or wool affair and with it she always wore stockings and a handbag over her arm. However, sometimes the Princess would choose to wear a pleated skirt and a crisp shirt-style blouse. If she were not going out to an official function, her jewelry would be no more than a double row of pearls around her neck and possibly a small sparkling brooch.

As endless fashion writers in the papers and slick magazines have pointed out so often, the Princess has wonderful dress sense. The writers knew how beautifully groomed she always looked when out on an engagement, but as I know, even when she did not intend going out of her sitting room for most of the day, she always changed her dress at least twice and never looked anything but lovely, stylish, and just right.

Margaret, as one would imagine of a Princess, never wore any of her clothes more than once without having them cleaned. After she had changed her day dress, for instance, it was sent immediately to be cleaned and pressed and then was hung away in her wardrobe and might not be worn again for six months, then be taken out, worn once more, then disposed of. If it was a particularly pretty one, the Princess might give Mrs. Gordon permission to take it away, but other times the dresses were sent out to charitable organizations.

I myself have more than once been ordered to take a

wardrobe to the head office of the Distressed Gentlefolks Association—an organization set up some years ago to help out those of the English landed gentry who were impoverished by crippling taxes and death duties. The Queen Mother was its patron. Naturally, the parcels I took were wrapped in quite ordinary paper and apart from the people I handed them to, no one knew they came from the wardrobe of the Princess. I used to speculate about which daughter of a once-proud stately home might be wearing a dress fit for a Princess—and what she might say if she knew.

Evening dresses were a different matter. After the Princess had worn them once for some official occasion they were returned to the makers, where they would be completely renovated and altered slightly in style so that by the time they came back, the Princess had virtually a new dress. But there too, she could not afford to be seen in it more than once again.

Incidentally, it is most interesting to remember one point about Her Royal Highness's wardrobe, which I found out quite by accident in talking to Mrs. Gordon. Like most other people, I had always imagined that the Princess, one of the world's leading fashion figures, would have been showered with free clothes from every fashion house in the world, all of them only too glad to have it discreetly known—for, of course, they could never advertise the fact— that their creations were being worn by Princess Margaret.

But I was surprised to learn that, in fact, the Princess paid for every stitch of the clothing she wore.

It was Mrs. Gordon who drew my attention to this one day when I was passing ten minutes having a quiet apéritif in her room. While I sat, Mrs. Gordon was busy selecting a suitable dress for the Princess to wear to a debutante ball that same night. I watched idly while she took out several, holding them to herself and looking at them critically in the mirror. Finally, she held up a gorgeous low-cut pale-blue sequined evening gown and studied it.

"That must have cost someone a pretty penny," I remarked.

To which Mrs. Gordon replied sharply: "It cost no one but the Princess herself. She pays for everything herself. People don't seem to realize that."

Which put me firmly in my place—but made me appreciative more of the Princess. After all, she had to budget for her clothes out of her allowance and at the same time was forced by the very nature of her position to buy only the best and to keep on buying to make sure that she was beyond criticism and comparison.

Apart from her dresses, the Princess's other clothes—the blouses, nightdresses and so on—were sent to a London laundry appointed by the Royal Household. They came weekly and took away a wicker basket in a laundry van which called at the back door of Clarence House. Mrs. Gordon herself washed Margaret's underclothes and flimsy things in the washbasin in Margaret's bathroom. It was not unusual for me, when sent on some errand to Her Royal Highness's bedroom, to find them hanging on a clotheshorse in front of an electric heater in the bedroom. The dresser would perform this job every day, and every day took a clean set in to the Princess while she was bathing.

Margaret liked to spend an hour or more in her bath in the mornings before coming back to the bedroom, where she sat at her dressing table to do her hair and make-up. These, she always did herself. Being a lovely young woman, she took great care with both her face and her hair and made an extremely good job of both. Even when she was going out on a big occasion, she applied her own powder, lipstick, eye shadow and eyebrow pencil and brushed her hair into the style she had chosen with the two big silver-backed hairbrushes she kept on the dressing table. Only very occasionally would she have her hairdresser call at Clarence House. Then he would be shown into her room, where he made the final adjustments to her coiffure, perhaps for the benefit of some really important state occasion.

On a routine day at Clarence House, the Princess would be ready to make her appearance downstairs by about 12:30. By this time, I had taken my own lunch break and eaten in the pantry along with the rest of the staff.

Shortly before the Princess came down, I made my way to the Royal elevator in the main corridor and waited by the door for the Princess. She was usually punctual, but she liked me always to be there in case there were any particular orders for me before the Princess took lunch.

The first signal of her arrival would be the gentle hum of the elevator as she stepped into it and descended.

Most mornings, Margaret would step from the elevator with a pleasant: "Good morning, John. What is the weather like today?" Or: "Will you come along to the sitting room please? There's something I want you to do." And off she strode, with me following behind her down the main corridor, and into the sitting room, the room in which she planned her life.

It was in these first few moments of every day that I could gauge Margaret's mood. The first words she spoke were the barometer of her temper.

If she had been out late and had not had her customary amount of sleep, then assuredly, she would not be in a sweet mood. My heart would sink if she stepped briskly out of the elevator, her head held high, glancing at me with a slight lift of an eyebrow but not a word before marching along to the sitting room. Then, I knew, things might be a little difficult. On really black days, she hurried into her room and gave the door a resounding slam. I knew the routine on days like this. I simply went back again to the pantry and waited for the indicator of the sitting room to ring for me. I never had to wait long. It was a fair guess that she would want a drink—vodka and orange juice it would be—but, suppressing a smile at the door, I tapped on it and went in. If it was vodka she wanted, I brought an unopened bottle and placed it on the tray alongside the orange juice, set out a glass and retired.

Just a short nip of this lethal drink, liberally laced with orange juice, would suffice her and she rapidly returned to her normal, pleasant self. Vodka and orange juice was one of her favorite drinks in the morning. Rather an eccentric choice, I always thought, but nevertheless a drink, as I have said, which had the power to snap the Princess out of one of her "moods."

But I was to find that the black days were generally few and far between. Princess Margaret is really one of the sweetest people I have ever met and I can honestly say that it was always—or very nearly always—a joy for me to work for her. Normally, she was full of high spirits in the morning and if she asked me to follow her to the sitting room, she liked to chatter easily and informally about anything and everything. She was quite inquisitive about the sort of things I did outside my work.

One morning, after I myself had had a pretty heavy night and had that "morning after" feeling, she looked at me closely with a mock frown and said impishly: "You are looking very tired this morning, John. Did you have a late night—or an early morning?"

I replied ruefully: "I am afraid I did, Your Royal Highness. I feel as if I could fall asleep on the clothesline."

She laughed and said: "Oh well, we all have to stick it out, don't we? But I, too, enjoy a bit of fun occasionally."

Thereafter, when I grew to know the Princess much better, we often exchanged wry glances when we both were feeling the effects of the night before. It was after exchanges such as this with my Princess that I realized she was beginning to accept me as something more than just an ordinary servant to whom her only comments might be nothing more than everyday instructions. I began to realize the significance of my Clarence House title, personal footman.

It was at such times that she would call me in on some pretext or other and talk to me about her previous evening's activities. I knew then that she must have really enjoyed herself and felt the human need to talk to somebody just as all people do when something particularly exciting has happened.

This usually occurred after a visit to the theatre—her favorite form of entertainment—with one or another of her current escorts. Princess Margaret was an intelligent critic who often looked down on the biased press notices of a play which she had seen and enjoyed, and she could always give a good reason why a play should be successful. I could be sure if a play was recommended to me by my Princess —and with the recommendation often went a couple of complimentary tickets—it would be worthwhile and I would enjoy it. Not many people can claim to have had a Princess for their guide to theatreland, but for me it was true.

On one occasion my Princess told me laughingly: "John, you really must go and see this film." She was talking about the screen version of the long-running West End play,

Espresso Bongo which she had been taken to see the previous evening.

I looked up when Margaret said this and listened attentively as usual to her expert opinions. "You will enjoy it, I'm sure." Then she added with a giggle: "I'm sure you will notice that Mother's mentioned."

I frowned and thought to myself, puzzled by this remark: *Mother's mentioned? What on earth did she mean?* But I said aloud: "Yes, Your Royal Highness, I'll take your word for it and go to to see it."

"I would like you to," said Margaret. And she urged me: "Go this evening. There will be nothing to keep you here. I am going out early, and no doubt you'll be back before I will, anyway."

So, happy to have been given this official leave of absence, I finished my work by five and went up to my room to change into my civilian clothes. Then, in happy-go-lucky mood, my evening chores forgotten, I strolled out of Clarence House and along to Haymarket and the Carlton cinema. I pulled my money out of my pocket and counted it. I had about two pounds left, but in Royal mood, I splashed out about an eighth of my weekly income on a twelve shillings-and-sixpenny ticket. I was led to the dress circle by a pretty young usherette, and on the way I asked her if she knew there had been a VIP in the cinema on the previous evening.

By coincidence, it was this very girl who had ushered my Princess and her party to their seats less than twenty-four hours before.

"I suppose you mean Princess Margaret," she said. I nodded, and with a glow of pride, told her: "Yes, she's my boss you know."

"In that case," said the usherette, "I think it is only right that you should use the same seat that Her Royal Highness sat in." She led me to a row near the front of the circle and, after asking a young couple if they would mind moving along, indicated where I should sit. I settled myself in the plush seat and sat back to enjoy the show.

The big film had only just started and I watched and listened with particular interest to see if I could tie up Margaret's remark about the Queen Mother with the racy dialogue.

The film was nearly halfway through before I found out what she had meant. Memory of her laughter prompted me to smile for a few seconds in understanding.

In the scene, Laurence Harvey, who played the part of a rock 'n' roll singer's rather dubious agent, was preparing himself for an important meeting with a famous impresario. The singer, played by Cliff Richard, was fussing around his agent and was made to say excitedly: "You will have to be elegant when you see this man." To which Harvey replied: "Look, who the bloody hell do you think I'm going to see, the Queen Mother?"

For the next two or three minutes the dialogue passed unheard. I was trying to picture how my Princess must have sat in this very seat trying hard to suppress what might have appeared to be her undignified giggles.

But I could well imagine the struggle she had. The comment in the film would have appealed greatly to Margaret's effervescent sense of humor.

After the show the lights went up and I stood for the National Anthem played as a background to a large picture of Margaret's sister, the Queen, looking rather solemnly at the audience. I couldn't help wondering how she would have reacted to this casual dig at their mother. Somehow, I had the feeling that she would not have accepted it with such good humor as my rather more lighthearted Princess.

I was about to leave the circle when the same usherette pushed her way through the crowd and came up to me. "Do tell me please," she said. "Did the Princess enjoy the film?" For a moment I was tempted to tell the girl just how much it had appealed to her and why. But my respect for the Princess and my special position with her curbed me, and I contented myself with replying simply: "She must have or she wouldn't have told me to come and see it."

She asked if the Princess had paid for my ticket but I told her: "No, not this time." The girl said: "Well, to you that does not matter, I suppose. You get a fortune in wages anyway, I bet." This made me smile, as I knew she probably earned twice as much as I did.

She obviously wanted to keep me in conversation and was terribly interested in what sort of person Margaret really was. To the public, who only saw her on show,

Margaret always appeared as a sort of fairy-tale Princess. But most people don't believe in fairy tales, and there have been times when I was off duty when I felt my blood boil to hear people make cheap and nasty remarks about Margaret.

Only too easily they believed she was a spoiled, pampered and petulant girl who had no knowledge of the world outside the Royal Palaces. Often I wanted to defend my Princess against these ill-mannered remarks. But I always felt that while in her service I would have to keep quiet and take it.

Of course, she wasn't a fairy Princess. Anyone who had seen her the morning after one of her late nights out could have told you that. But she was a lovely and innocent young woman who didn't deserve the harsh and often spiteful comments that were made against her by less lucky and more envious women.

All this skipped through my mind as I looked at the young cinema usherette, her face betraying the eagerness with which she had greeted my earlier remarks about my Royal mistress. I knew that whatever I told her would be repeated and probably embroidered to her circle of friends and would eventually lead to just another distorted story about Margaret's "goings on" at the House. So I made my excuse and walked out through the theatre crowds into the night and back to the quiet of Clarence House, to await the return of my Princess. I was in plenty of time. She came back in the early hours, and I had to sit up and read a book until I heard her return. Frequently I had to sit up and wait for the Princess. I didn't mind that, but the most infuriating thing was that more often than not, she would make straight for the elevator and go up to bed without calling me, which meant that my time had been wasted. Still, that was all part of my life with Princess Margaret.

For *Espresso Bongo* I bought my own ticket, but on the meager salary I received at Clarence House—and believe me, this was common to all Royal Servants—I could not afford frequent visits to the expensive London cinemas and theatres. It it hadn't been for Margaret I could not possibly have kept abreast of current films and plays. Incidentally, my Princess had nothing whatever to do with the salary I earned at Clarence House. We had to thank Lord Adam Gordon—who kept a very tight rein on the Queen Mother's pursestrings—for the uncompetitive figures which appeared on our monthly pay-checks.

It is regarded as a privilege in Britain to work for the Royal Family and something which is above mere money. But it has its drawbacks. For instance, it was often difficult for a former Royal servant to find subsequent employment on leaving the Household. It has always been the opinion—a completely false one, from my experience—of the British aristocracy and the richer upper classes that servants have been made lazy by a spell in Royal employ. "Life," they say, with a knowing nod, "has been made much too easy for these people and habits are hard to break." And I have known applications for employment from other former Royal servants to end up in the wastepaper basket for this very reason.

Maybe the Princess realized how difficult it was for me to make ends meet, for when I went into the sitting room in the mornings in response to her call, she might often walk over to her desk without a word and come back and hand me a pair of tickets for some show or other which had been sent to Clarence House for her. But, for reasons of policy, she never used these tickets and she would hand them to me and say: "Here you are, John, perhaps you can make use of these."

One of the finest shows I saw by courtesy of the Princess was *West Side Story*. She herself had seen it something like four times, and she treasured the long-playing record of the show, which was often on her record player. When I saw the show, I appreciated why she went back so many times. The excitement, the verve and the compulsive rhythms were made to fit the Princess's personality exactly.

But back to the routine of Princess Margaret's day: I used to get my instructions when I was summoned to the sitting room when she came downstairs soon after noon. One of the first things Her Royal Highness did was to riffle through her desk diary in which she had entered her forthcoming engagements. While I stood by her desk, the Princess would give me a rough idea of what her day would be—whether she would be going out after lunch, in for tea, or going out in the evening, and I made a mental note of the sorts of things I would have to arrange.

But Margaret had another way of letting me know what was on the "menu" for the day, namely by leaving me little notes on her own special notepaper. These got left on her desk or the drink tray and would contain these instructions. She might want the car ordered early in the morning, something collected from a West End shop or perhaps a trip to the drugstore with a roll of film for developing. Later in my service, this job would involve a journey to the studio-flat of Mr. Antony Armstrong-Jones in Pimlico with a roll or two of film with perhaps a sealed note taped to them.

But in the early days of my service, Mr. Armstrong-Jones—later to figure so largely in my life with the Princess—had not yet come into the picture, as it were! But all the time I knew the Princess, she had been a very keen photographer. She loved to take pictures of the Royal Family and the dogs, and of guests who had been invited to stay with the Family on one or another of their country estates at Windsor, Sandringham or Balmoral. Margaret had two cameras which she took with her whenever she went away. They were a French miniature 35MM type and a Japanese-made reflex. Later, when Mr. Armstrong-Jones was a regular visitor at Clarence House, they spent hours talking and comparing photographs, and many is the time I have watched Tony giving Margaret instructions and hints on the way to take a certain picture for the best effect. Indeed, it is safe to say that it was their cameras which helped launch the romance which was later to shake the whole world. But more of this later.

By the time I had taken my daily orders from the Princess, it was almost one o'clock. After I left her, Margaret liked to sort through the morning's mail, slitting open the envelopes with her desk paper-knife. Then, shortly after one, she left the sitting room, walked down the corridor into the main hallway where directly opposite her was the door leading into the ornate morning room. By the time she entered, her lunch companions—always the same people unless there was an official lunch scheduled—would be assembled and waiting for her and the Queen Mother. This, by the way, was the only time of the day when the Queen

Mother met her daughter officially. Apart from lunch, they lived their lives in the same house entirely separately. Only on very rare occasions—one memorable one about which I shall tell you a great deal more later—did they take tea together.

I never quite understood the reason for this, for Margaret and her mother were quite close. I suppose it was simply that the demands of their public lives pulled in opposite directions. When one was at home, the other might be out on official business, and vice-versa. The Queen Mother, of course, probably took her official duties rather more seriously than Margaret, although both of them were strongly aware of the importance of their jobs. And, of course, it was and is a job of work which they had to do. It required a good deal of effort and preparation for them whenever they had to go on an engagement. They had to study up on the people or organization they were going to meet, always had to smile even though they might feel dreadful, and always had to appear interested even though they might be crushingly bored. It was a job which required good health and considerable stamina, and I know that they would go out to perform their duty unfailingly unless they really were laid low. I knew that an announcement saying that either of them could not attend a function because they were indisposed meant consierably more than that.

If only more people realized that the Royal Family does have to work hard at its job—and a good deal harder than many, we might hear a little less of the sniping at them which is the favorite occupation of certain people of all ranks and walks of life.

However, if they had both escaped official functions for the day, they would take lunch together. Their companions were all members of the Clarence House official staff, who assembled in the morning room shortly before one, helping themselves to drinks and talking shop. They arrived from their offices in different parts of the House: Princess Margaret's Lady in Waiting, the Honorable Iris Peake, who was at Margaret's side whenever and wherever there was a public function to perform. Then there was the man who recommended me for the job, Lord Adam Gordon, the Comptroller. Also Her Royal Highness's official voice, her press secretary Major John Griffin. Why they ever bothered to have a press secretary I could hardly imagine. For one thing, I got the impression that Major Griffin disliked most of the press, and for another, when he did talk to them he spent most of his time denying the constantly recurring rumors in the world's newspapers that the Princess was to marry Lord What-Not, or the Marquis of This-and-That or any of the others she might have been photographed with at some obscure outing.

With them were usually two of the Queen Mother's personal staff, her Lady in Waiting and her private secretary, Colonel Martin Gilliat, who has been in her service for years and probably knows more about the affairs of the Royal Family than anyone outside the Family itself.

When lunch was imminent, I took up my position behind the door linking the morning room with the library, where lunch was taken on such informal occasions.

The morning room was a large one, airy and bright in summer, but tending to be a little chilly in winter. It was tastefully furnished in pale blue and cream and measured about sixteen feet by twenty-four, and as Margaret came into the room this is how it looked:

Directly opposite the door leading from the corridor were three large windows hung with pale blue satin drapes which looked out on to the private road leading from St. James's to the Mall, the tree-lined avenue which stretches from Trafalgar Square right up to the entrance to Buckingham Palace.

On the right-hand wall of the room about four steps from the doorway was a very large double doorway through which the luncheon party passed in to the library. At the opposite end of the room from the library one could look out through a tall French window which opened out onto the main driveway near the big gate of Clarence House.

The French windows were flanked by pots of flowers, and there were more flowers in bloom in the long, narrow window boxes.

Adjacent to the door was a magnificent marble fire-place with a large mantle above it. On the wall over this hung a big mirror in an ornate gilded rectangular frame.

On either side there were smaller mirrors and two more were hung on the wall between the windows. But probably the loveliest thing in the room was the huge crystal chandelier suspended from the ceiling. When it was on it reflected in all the mirrors in the room, giving a rich warm glow which never failed to delight strangers who were invited into the morning room, which also served as the waiting room.

I suppose this was the reason why there were so many mirrors in the room—so that the women could titivate, and the men straighten their ties.

Across the corners of the room on either side of the French windows were the typical high-backed settees of which the Queen Mother seemed so fond.

These were of Regency style covered in pale blue satin to match the curtains. I always found these settees—often I would sit down for a few seconds when no one was in the room to take a short rest—more ornamental than comfortable.

Beneath the windows opposite the door stood two mahogany tables, one of which bore the drink tray with its generous decanters of gin, sherry, and orange juice and the special sealed bottle of Scotch from which Margaret would have her pre-lunch Scotch and Malvern water.

The only other furniture in the room was two armchairs facing each other on either side of the fireplace, with two tiered occasional tables next to them and two other small tables, on opposite sides of the library door.

All around the room on every available table stood vases packed with flowers. A good many of these were sent up twice a week in huge bunches from the flowerbeds of Windsor Castle. The rest of the occasional decorations were placed on the mantlepiece. On either end of it was a very large flowered porcelain vase and in the middle a heavy brass chiming clock.

Also on the mantlepiece was a porcelain caricature of one of the Royal Family's favorite people, Sir Winston Churchill. He dominated the room with his pugnacious jaw and inevitable cigar. Strangely enough, I never saw Sir Winston at Clarence House, although the Queen Mother and Princess Margaret met him very frequently during his active life and even occasionally when he came out of his retirement to attend a public engagement.

This was the scene when the Princess and the Queen Mother came down for lunch. In the easy informal atmosphere one of the gentlemen would do the honors and pour the Queen Mother a modest gin and tonic, and for the Princess a Scotch and Malvern Water.

They were all standing and the conversation would flow

easily. The party had time for just one drink together before a page came into the room to announce that lunch was ready, in the library.

After the announcement he slid open the communicating doors. As I have said, I would already be in the library waiting to serve at table.

The party waited until the Queen Mother moved towards the library, then led by her and the Princess they would stroll, still talking animatedly, into the library and take their places behind the chairs set out around the full-sized circular table in the center of the room.

Before sitting one of the gentlemen, usually Lord Adam, would say a simple Grace and then I would help the Princess into her chair. The Queen Mother was attended by her personal footman.

After seating my Princess, I took up my position behind her chair and waited until the party was quite ready to begin lunch.

The library was also an elegant room lit by another of those huge and lovely chandeliers. Directly underneath it was the round table. Bookcases covered the lower part of three walls of the library, and on the fourth wall to the left as one entered from the morning room, were two big windows which presented a similar view out over the private road with its big gates at each end. Between the windows was a marble table. In the far left-hand corner of the room was a standard lamp. Apart from these items, the room was furnished only by the rows and rows of expensive leather-bound books standing stiffly in the bookcases.

I rarely had time to inspect the books, but from the titles I did see, they seemed to be mainly concerned with the history of England and were lengthy textbooks about the Kings and Queens of England, going back to the year one. No one, to my knowledge, ever read any of them, and they might well have been dummies, but they made a fine array around the room.

However, lunchtime was no time to think about books, for I and the other Royal servants were kept far too busy constantly trying to anticipate the demands of the party and making sure they never had to break off their conversation to call for anything. We took turns to dash down to the basement kitchen fifty yards away through the sliding doors at the other end of the library, across the dining room proper—reserved for official luncheons and dinners—out into the corridor and down the hollow-sounding wooden stairs to the kitchens. It was quite a trot and took almost ten minutes by the time one had collected the trayful of food and hurried as quickly as safety would allow up the stairs, into the dining room and, slowing down to a more dignified walk, into the library. There was no hotplate in the library, so the food had to be served just as it arrived and it never seemed to be as piping hot as one might have expected of a Royal lunch.

Conversation at lunch usually settled down to a discussion of the routine of the Clarence House working day or the details of forthcoming engagements, although if Margaret was in a particularly playful mood, she would entertain the whole table with witty comments about the functions she had attended and the people of all types that she had met.

Her characterizations of some of the more pompous officials she had been introduced to were terribly accurate portrayals of the typical British "committee" types who throw themselves into local public life, not because they have any particular gift for administration, but because it bolsters their egos. I suppose it is the same the world over, but for me there is something irresistibly funny about stationmasters, whose routine job assumes huge importance if someone like the Princess passes through. So often, I have seen these people puff up like penguins in the reflected glory of Royalty. Everything and everyone is swept out of the path for the big occasion and they usually bring out some awful, affected little speech to greet the Royal traveler. If only they could have known how much the Princess hated this kind of affectation and how mercilessly she lampooned them whenever she got on the subject!

Sometimes at lunch these high-spirited outbursts from my Princess would bring a murmur of "Oh, Margaret, really," from the Queen Mother and meaningful smiles would be exchanged between the officials at the table. But Margaret would shrug and smile sweetly and accept the gentle reprimand in good humor.

Now and then, the subject of politics would crop up, particularly if there had been some big world event in the papers that morning. But the Queen Mother, anxiously correct at all times, would hastily change the subject, for it was a golden, unbreakable rule of Royal protocol that never, never must they give an opinion on current politics. It was all rooted in history—when parliament fought a bitter battle to throw off the interference from the throne. And this later became an unwritten rule that was never broken except perhaps on the most intimate occasions.

Lunch was served in an informal manner from silver dishes, and the company, including the Queen Mother and the Princess helped themselves to whatever they fancied. Margaret always took a generous helping of meat but, perhaps because she, like most other handsome young women, was conscious of her figure, she always refused potatoes. I always offered them to her and she brushed them aside, sometimes saying with a reluctant frown: "You know I never take them, John." But apart from this one fad, the Princess was a good eater.

Lunch normally consisted of four courses including fruit and half a dozen different varieties of native and Continental cheeses. It was always accompanied by a considerable amount of wine—about half a bottle each—which had been chosen at the steward's discretion, although for some reason, white wine was always served, never red, no matter what was on the menu.

The menu, by the way, was chosen either by the Queen Mother or the Princess. Before lunch, they would skim through a suggested selection of menus and check whatever they thought they would like. The others ate what the Royal couple chose. As I think I have mentioned before, I never had any great opinion of the Clarence House kitchens or cuisine. Somehow, the food didn't seem to be as well cooked or garnished with the care I might have imagined would be the standard for a part of the Royal Household. Nevertheless, lunch always went well and no one to my knowledge ever complained about it. They spent a little over an hour at the meal, the progress of which was timed by the speed with which the Queen Mother ate, for, of course, no new course was served before Her Majesty had quite finished the previous one.

When dessert was served, my Princess would refuse it and

light up one of her favorite brand of cigarettes while the others ate. It was just the Princess's habit and everyone accepted it without comment. One of the gentlemen present would be ready to offer Margaret a light from his lighter.

By 2:15 they would rise. The Princess might ask me to come along to the sitting room at 2:30, or might walk through without a word and ring for me a few minutes later. After lunch, Margaret had the afternoon to herself and spent a couple of hours catching up with her diary or bringing her photograph album up to date.

The Princess had a lovely leather bound album for her photographs, most of which she had taken herself. She could spend hours slotting the prints into the pages, captioning them with a place and a date. Most of the pictures were of her family, her dogs or of one of the Royal homes. She was an excellent craftswoman with the camera and some of her pictures were really first-class. She must have admired the work of Mr. Armstrong-Jones long before they met, for he was really coming into a leading place among the world's photographers and his work could hardly have escaped the notice of Margaret, the enthusiastic amateur. The Princess was particularly good at "freezing" her dogs on film when she snapped them while she exercised them in one of the public parks like Green Park or St. James's—which were both one minute from Clarence House on either side of the Mall.

The Royal Family in England is not so free-and-easy as some of the more informal thrones such as Holland and Norway where members of the Families mingle quite freely with the public. But many, many times, Margaret has passed unnoticed in the parks, wearing only a suit and headscarf and strolling with her three dogs scampering around her heels. And I think my Princess enjoyed these moments, free of her responsibilities, when she could walk out of her home without the attention of hundreds of eyes on her.

One of the other jobs Margaret had in the afternoons was to rehearse the speeches she had to make. The afternoon before an official engagement, she spent writing and speaking and correcting until the speech was the way she wanted it. Not that she had very much scope. Bound as she was by officialdom, she had to conform more or less to the standard speech for the opening of a building, the inspection of a school, or the launching of a ship. But she did at least have the satisfaction of writing the speech herself—after being given the outline of what it was she was supposed to be doing—and she took considerable pains to insure that it fell smoothly and intelligently on the ear. A phrase here, a word there, could make the difference between boredom and acceptance.

I used to keep in touch with the Princess during the afternoon and to make sure that everything was always to her satisfaction, I would go to Margaret's sitting room two or three times. Perhaps it was only to dust off the tables, water the flowers or put a few books straight, but if there was anything that the Princess wanted me for, it saved her the trouble of ringing for me. And, very often, I could hear her small, feminine voice in rehearsal.

When the Princess grew accustomed to my presence, she began to ask my opinion of her speeches.

One time I heard her talking as I rounded the corner of the corridor, and as I approached her door, I guessed what she was doing. I tapped softly on the door and went in. Margaret was walking slowly up and down the middle of the room reading aloud from the sheaf of notes she held up before her in her hand. In a clear voice she addressed the room, congratulating it on the new addition to a provincial hospital. She glanced across at me as I entered the room, then continued speaking. She carried on for a minute or two, then stopped by the fireplace, turned and said: "It now gives me great pleasure to declare this building open."

With that, she dropped her hand with the notes in it to her side and asked brightly: "Well, John, what did you think of that?"

I replied: "Perfectly all right, Your Royal Highness."

But she did not seem to be impressed since I could hardly say that it sounded terrible. Actually, it was quite a reasonable piece, but Margaret was definitely not satisfied. I went on dusting the tables and putting the flowers straight while the Princess walked slowly and thoughtfully over to her desk. After a few moments of concentration, she picked up a pen and scratched vigorously at the writing on the last sheet. Finally, she sighed, her mind made up. She walked back to the fireplace and stood with her back to it and said aloud once more: "Now I have great pleasure in declaring this magnificent building open."

She smiled and asked: "Now, that's a bit better, isn't it?" Without waiting for a reply, went over to the desk and placed the notes in readiness for the following day.

We both knew well enough it was not far from the kind of stilted phrase delivered in a thousand speeches every year by the Royals on duty, but it was all that the VIP's wanted.

In such ways the Princess passed her afternoon until about 4:30. Then it would be time for tea. I had to bring it to her in the sitting room on a tray covered with a fresh white cloth. I set it up on a small table in the center of the room and placed one of the dainty high-backed chairs beside it. Margaret usually took a pot of scented China tea, which I always prepared personally, a plate of paté de fois gras sandwiches and two or three fancy cakes. She was usually alone for tea, as was the Queen Mother, who had her tea in her sitting room on the first floor.

By the time tea was ready, Margaret might be resting on one of the settees, reading perhaps, or relaxing completely to the accompaniment of a stereo recording. The preparation and serving of tea was little more than the playing out of a ritual, for more often than not, nothing on the tray would be touched when I came back to the room to clear it away. If she was in the room when I came in to take away the untouched things, I might hesitate, making a mute inquiry whether she had really finished, and my Princess would say something like: "All right, John. I just didn't feel hungry." She would probably be thinking about the evening ahead. The Princess was a gregarious person and preferred to have people around her and I think that one afternoon on her own was quite enough. By 5:30, she would be perfectly ready to go up to her room to make a change of dress and start getting ready for the arrival of her guests, or escort.

Of course, she would be in her element when it came to putting on new clothes and making herself pretty for the evening. With the help and advice of the faithful Mrs. Gordon, the Princess selected a dress—either a simple cocktail affair for the more casual social occasion or, for a big evening, one of the flamboyant, billowing evening gowns which she was able to wear to such wonderful advantage. With a change of shoes and her matching assessories laid out for her, Margaret would sit once more before her own reflection in her dressing table mirror and make herself up and carefully comb her hair into position.

Chapter Five

Evening at Clarence House began with the descent of Princess Margaret from her bedroom, changed, made-up and invigorated by the prospect of an evening out with her friends. It might be a visit to the theatre, a night club, a private reception, a party, or just a quiet social evening. But no matter what it was, Margaret was lit up with the excitement of a person who could find fun from life, whatever the occasion.

By the time she came down in the elevator, I had cleared away the tea things and had prepared the evening drink tray and placed it in the sitting room, ready for Margaret and her visitors.

When I first went into the service of Her Royal Highness, I might have thought that the preparation of a tray of drinks was a pretty routine thing, but I soon found that it was an item that Margaret paid particular attention to. She had the habit of inspecting the tray to see that it was quite in order. Chief object of her scrutiny was the special bottle of sealed Malvern water, a kind of distilled natural spring water from the hills of England's West Country, which the Princess insisted on taking with her Scotch whisky. Later I will tell you about some of the difficulties which arose out of this particular little foible. Margaret never drank anything in the evenings but whisky and Malvern water.

Despite all I have read about the Princess' drinking champagne whenever she could, I never knew her to take that drink unless it was when she was obliged to on a rare, special occasion.

For the half hour or so before her guests arrived, my Princess usually liked to sit quietly and smoke, with the record player making sweet music. Now and then, she would get up and swirl around the room, making her dress rustle as she moved. She was quite without affectation, and if I happened to be in the room when she was practicing a dance step or two, then she just went on without feeling my presence to be any affront to her dignity.

I think this lack of Royal frostiness was one of the things I loved most about my Princess. It took time to get to understand her, for she was a curious mixture of the Princess who knew and understood her duty to the Throne and accepted her work for the Crown as part of her life, and the lovely young woman with a personality all her own—an intelligent and forthright girl with opinions of her own and a determination not to let Royal protocol interfere too much with her life—providing she was off duty. On top of this, she had a natural charm and grace which made it difficult for her to be distant with anyone, even her personal footman!

When I entered service at Clarence House, I wondered if the picture I had built up in my mind of the Princess as a warmhearted creature would prove to be a false one.

It most definitely was not.

Sometimes the Princess would spend an evening alone in Clarence House, and at such times, she would relax completely. I can remember the evenings when I have walked into her sitting room to find her lounging on a settee with her feet up and a shoe kicked off a few yards away, making no attempt to move as I entered.

One time, she was lying full-length on the settee, her head pillowed on two pink brocade cushions and her dark hair spread out around her face. Her eyes were closed and she was concentrating on the music—a newly-released record— her cigarette holder describing a dreamy accompaniment to the melody.

Unconsciously, I started to hum the tune softly, and without opening her eyes, Margaret murmured: "Isn't this music delightful?"

"Yes, it's wonderful, Your Royal Highness," I answered, looking down at her.

She looked her very loveliest, lying there in a midnight blue sequined cocktail dress with a tight bodice and flared skirt. She was lightly made up, her powder and lipstick applied with the delicate touch of an expert. Her shoulders

above the low-cut neckline shone silkily in the soft lights.
On the table by her side stood a half-glass of whisky and
water and in the ashtray there were two or three inch-long
stubs. She lay perfectly still, lost in the atmosphere of the
romantic music, her eyes closed, her face serene. I stood
there for a few seconds, inwardly moved by the sight of this
lovely sleeping beauty. Then I turned and withdrew, tactfully
forgetting the mission which had brought me to the room.

If she stayed in, Princess Margaret usually found a book to
amuse her. She read all manner of things, mostly novels in
popular paperback form. She propped herself up on the settee with plenty of cushions, the drinks and the cigarettes
near at hand, until about 8 o'clock, when I served her a
simple supper in the sitting room. She took it on one of the
coffee tables and was fond of eating casually with just a fork
—American-style—and continued reading with the book
propped up on the table. She never took wine with this meal,
but would sometimes pour herself a whisky and water. Often,
quite absorbed in her book, she pushed aside the plate and
sat reading at the table with a frown of concentration across
her face. When I entered, she rose without a word and
walked, still reading, across to the settee again. She might
ask me to switch on a lamp, or draw the curtains, but during
the evenings her demands were small.

It would be 11:30 or 12 before she thought of going to
bed. When she was ready, she would ring for me and when
I answered the summons, Margaret was up and ready to leave
the room. "I'm off to bed now, John," she would say. "Collect your animals and you can go to bed. Good-night." And
out she walked. After clearing up quickly, I ushered the
Princess's dogs into the garden for their last call, herded
them up to my room and bedded the four of us down. Five
hundred yards away, on the other side of the building, Margaret would be settling down in her bedroom.

I was one of the very few servants who ever saw the
Princess's bedroom. She would often send me up to get a
jewel case or some item she particularly wanted to take
with her on a trip, and once the Princess and myself were
used to each other, she had no second thoughts about
sending me up on such errands to her innermost sanctuary.

High up in the building, the bedroom was in a perfect
position, commanding a wonderful panoramic view from the

windows at one corner of Clarence House—of St. James's Park, the Mall and, across the treetops in the distance, a full view of Buckingham Palace, the home of her sister, Queen Elizabeth.

The room, naturally, was utterly feminine, decorated in a lovely restful shade of pale pink which gave it a warm cosiness. The air in the room was constantly tinged with the slightest hint of expensive perfume which was unmistakably Margaret. As I have already described, the room is at the end of the long corridor on the second floor which leads from the staircase to the front of the House.

Imagine, now, that you are with me as we walk up the main staircase and into the bedroom. It is deserted now, of course, but has been prepared for the Princess to retire.

We tread the thick carpet of the corridor silently, with only the occasional creak of a floorboard to tell we are there. The air is warm, the corridor spotless. We walk to the very end of the corridor, where, on the right, is the cream door opening into the room.

The first thing we notice on entering is the simplicity of it. Tasteful, charming and not at all cluttered. The room is dominated by the large double bed, its highly polished dark wooden headboard against the wall behind the door. The 5-foot tall Princess has chosen a 6 foot, 4 inch bed topped by a foam-rubber mattress, firm but yielding gently to the touch. The sheets are of white cotton, trimmed around the edges with a pastel shade of colored lace. There are two pillows, one on top of the other, well puffed up and sheathed in pillow-cases which match the sheets.

The rest of the bed is covered by a luxurious heavy pink silk eiderdown and folded back across the bottom of the bed is the vivid pink coverlet, touching the floor at either side. It looks the sort of bed that would guarantee a good night's sleep.

And just to complete the picture, Mrs. Gordon has already laid out one of the Princess's flimsy, full-length nylon nighties.

On either side of the bed is a low four-legged polished table. On each stands a small bedside lamp with a delicate pink silk shade edged with a lace frill. Switched on, the lamps cast a soft light throughout the room, sufficient to read by, but not hurtful to the eyes. Within easy reach of Margaret as she lies in bed, are a silver ashtray and a small radio, cased in a blue star-speckled material. These have been placed on the left-hand table from the bed. To the right, she has a light brown pigskin photograph case. It is on the table near the lamp. Look closer and you will see that the case contains three small head-and-shoulders portraits of a man. You recognize him. And you will not be surprised when I say that to me, they constitute one of the most significant things I encountered during my service with Princess Margaret. But more of that later. . . .

Behind the pigskin case and the lamp on this table you will notice the two telephones. One, a cream-colored instrument, is a direct line through to the Queen at Buckingham Palace. It is the most inaccessible of the two, for I do not think it was used too often. The other, a standard black telephone, is a normal outside line through the Clarence House switchboard.

Across the oyster-pink fitted carpet, in the wall opposite the bed, are three windows draped in pink satin curtains. Peep through the curtains and you will look down onto the Mall to the left, with Buckingham Palace at the end of it. Between the windows are a large cream wardrobe and a waist-high chest of drawers in which are kept the Princess's handkerchiefs, stockings and underclothes.

Across the top of the chest is a little white lace runner. On it is a small round luminous clock flanked by two photographs. They are of the late King George VI and the former Queen Elizabeth, now the Queen Mother. They, of course, are Margaret's parents. Not very remarkable photos, either of them, but ones that the Princess treasures and which are indicative of her very real affection for her parents.

On the far side of the room beyond the bed are two more windows which look out over the garden of Clarence House, and across the Mall to the beautiful St. James's Park. Between the windows we can see the kidney-shaped dressing table at which the Princess does her make-up and her hair. It is fitted with three mirrors, a large rectangular one in the center and an adjustable hinged mirror on either side.

The sides of this ultra-feminine affair are curtained in pink and white chintz, and a low stool in front of the table is covered in the same material.

The glass top of the table is littered with the bric-a-brac

of a woman's make-up requisites—as on millions of dressing tables all over the world in palaces and humble cottages.

Let us take a closer look. We can see a collection of nail files, jars of face cream, tubes of lipstick, and a brush set comprising two green bone-backed brushes edged in gold, and a hand mirror in the same material. Next to them Margaret has thrown an ordinary comb. Also lying there is a half-filled packet of tissues which she uses for removing her make-up at night. In the morning there will be half a dozen of them smeared with lipstick and powder tossed on the dressing table.

To the left of the table in the corner of the bedroom there is another chest of drawers. More photographs are displayed here, this time some which the Princess has taken herself, of the Queen, Prince Philip and the Royal children, Prince Charles and Princess Anne—Andrew, the second Prince, had not yet been born.

Notice how informal these pictures are. They are just family snaps taken in Scotland, one showing Prince Philip proudly wearing the kilt, with the Queen at his side. The other is of the children in traditional Scottish dress of tartan kilts and tweed jackets. The Family always took to their heavy kilts whenever they went up for their annual holiday to the Castle of Balmoral, their official Scottish residence. They always looked forward eagerly to this trip and entered into the Highland spirit with great zest.

But now let us turn and look back across Margaret's bedroom towards the door. We see facing us a second wardrobe much larger than the other and with a full-length mirror in the door. It stands against the far wall, and to the right of it is the door leading into the Princess's bathroom.

This, then, is the bedroom, charming in its simplicity and reflecting accurately the feminine grace of my Princess. Let us go now through the connecting door from the bedroom to the bathroom. Once through the door we find ourselves in a narrow connecting passageway about four steps long. A blank wall faces us, but at the end and to the left is another door which opens directly into the bathroom itself. Open it, and we step into the perfumed atmosphere of the Royal bathroom.

Beneath our feet is a fitted carpet in the same oyster pink that covered the bedroom floor. The toilet is situated in the far left-hand corner and to the right is the modern white porcelain bath. It has two chromium-plated taps at one end with a chrome plug on a tiny chain. There is no shower as such, but in one of the lockers of the bathroom there is a rubber tubing hand shower which can be plugged into the taps.

Resting across the bath is a tray, also in chrome, with compartments in it containing colored scented soaps, a sponge or two and a long-handled loofah. Plenty of mirrors everywhere, you see, and there is another on an adjustable arm fixed above the soap tray. The bathroom is faced with white tiles all around up to shoulder level and set into the walls are little glass shelves on which Margaret keeps her bath salts and perfumes. On the left-hand wall, draped over a hot water rail is the Princess's bathmat.

Next to this is the white handbasin, complete with soap and a small nail brush and a face flannel draped over the side. Above the basin is a square mirror and on either side of this a white-painted bathroom cabinet. The bathroom is brightly lit with a powerful bulb suspended from the ceiling in a white frosted glass shade.

Chapter Six

I have described a day in the life of Princess Margaret as it affected me. Now in this and in later chapters I want to put down some of the fascinating detail of my life with the Princess. But I hope it will be clear that my duties as personal footman to Her Royal Highness extended from the very beginning to the very end of her day. Because of this I was to know her as well as anyone outside the Royal Family and the intimate circle of friends which were dubbed the Margaret Set. I am very proud to recall that the Princess came to accept me as a part of her life and revealed to me some of the spontaneous warmth of the lovely girl behind the mask of Royalty.

I am proud that I became part of Margaret's life even for a comparatively short time. Where she went, I went, always on hand to see her go out, whether it be for an evening of relaxation or a morning of official duty, and always on hand to welcome her back.

As I have said, official engagements were part of the demands made on Margaret and all the other members of the Royal Family in return for their Royal position. Many of them were pleasant-enough chores but obviously the thrill of visiting schools, addressing umpteen societies, visiting factories and laying foundation stones would quickly pall.

And I'm afraid that sometimes on her return to Clarence House after one of these outings Margaret would not be able to disguise her expression of gloom or outright relief. It sometimes happened that the Queen Mother would come down to the front door to see her daughter return.

I well remember one rather revealing incident, which amused me very much indeed. It was a sullen rainy day.

The Princess had been driven back from some tedious function and was greeted by the Queen Mother who waited with
me just inside the half-open main door of Clarence House.
The dogs had just been let out into the garden for a run.

As sweetly as ever the Queen Mother greeted Margaret.
"Hello, darling," she said. "Did you enjoy yourself?"

Margaret scowled and sighed: "Honestly Mother, I was
bored stiff."

The Queen Mother raised her eyebrows in surprise, threw
me a glance and said confidentially to the Princess: "Never
mind, darling, you must always remember to look interested
even if you are not."

But Margaret was not impressed. She huffed her shoulders
and stomped off down the corridor leaving the Queen Mother looking after her with the glimmer of a smile round her
mouth. It occurred to me that perhaps she remembered her
younger days when banquets and official functions seemed
relentlessly boring. She stood there, wistfully, for a few moments, then called the dogs back and went up again to her
room. Margaret went straight to the sitting room and a few
minutes later, I heard the music from her record-player
drifting through the closed door. Music was an essential part
of Margaret's life and she put records on to suit all kinds of
moods. I suppose it soothed her. On this occasion, I think she
called on Frank Sinatra—one of her favorite artists—to
calm her down.

The brief meeting between Margaret and the Queen Mother was one of the comparatively few times when the mother
and daughter met, apart from lunchtime, during the day at
the House.

To communicate during the day, both the Princess and the
Queen Mother were able to call one another on the House
service telephone. They had only to pick it up in their sitting rooms, dial the right code-number and they were automatically connected. This system also connected to my room
and to the apartments and offices of the rest of the House
staff. But somehow, both the Princess and the Queen Mother
seemed a little shy of using the telephone. They preferred
to contact each other by means of little notes carried by
hand. The notes were sealed in small envelopes and addressed, very formally it seemed to me, to either "Her
Majesty, Queen Elizabeth" or "Her Royal Highness, Princess

Princess Margaret and the Queen Mother, dressed for the Coronation, in the Throne Room at Buckingham Palace.

David John Payne opens a car door for his Princess.

Frequently called upon to make grueling personal appearances, (above) the Princess hands trophy to Lord Cowdray at the Goodwood Week Polo Tournament. (Below) The Princess receives film stars Sophia Loren and William Holden at a premiere at the Odeon Theatre in Leicester Square, London.

Peter Townsend and the Princess were close friends when he accompanied the Royal Family as equerry on a tour of Africa in 1947. But in 1955 Margaret renounced all hope of marrying the divorced RAF group Captain.

WIDE WORLD

Billy Wallace, formerly one of the Princess's favorite escorts, was the man with whom she went out the night she learned that Peter Townsend had become engaged to Marie Luce.

RUSSELL SEDGWICK FROM PIX

Official duties take Margaret to such far corners of the world as Tanganyika. She chats with Tribal Chief known as the Mangi Mkuu of Chagga.

WIDE WORLD

Tony, with the help of his petite assistant, displays some ski clothes he designed.

WIDE WORLD

Margaret." It always seemed a bit stilted to address them like that. They would even write their initials on the bottom left-hand corner of the envelopes.

I have already remarked on the direct-line telephone linking Clarence House with Buckingham Palace. There was one, you remember, in Princess Margaret's bedroom. Others were in her sitting room and in the Queen Mother's apartments.

So much for communications. I mention them in passing. But I must say that for a large part of her life, Margaret was distinctly out of contact with the other members of the Royal Family. I refer to her evenings. The sort of soirée that I have mentioned was a comparatively isolated event. By far her favorite way of spending an evening was to head for the bright lights of London's West End where the theatres, clubs and night life in general were concentrated. Often in a party, usually escorted by a particular gentleman, Margaret would sweep gaily out of Clarence House in the early evening and return quite often in the early hours of the morning.

The escorts were, in the main, one of the three regulars who were far and away leaders in the Margaret popularity stakes—Billy Wallace, the Mayfair millionaire man-about-town; the handsome Dominic Elliott, son of a Scottish Earl; and the young Lord Plunkett, Deputy Master of the Household to Her Majesty the Queen.

All these were acceptable in every sense to the hierarchy of the Family and at various times during my service at Clarence House, their names were linked romantically with Margaret's.

After an evening at the theatre—their tickets obtained discreetly through a booking agency—the whole lot of them might come back to Clarence House, tumbling out of their cars laughing and calling out to each other, and stream into Margaret's sitting room. They might even decide to have a little late dinner. These decisions were always a thorn in my side, for they never thought about it until 11 o'clock or so, which meant I had to wait up all evening, and then stay up to serve dinner at midnight. Thereafter, I would be expected to remain up until Margaret turned in, maybe at two, three or four in the morning.

Dinner for the Margaret Set was served with full honors in

the official state dining room—with all the trimmings. But they were always terribly gay affairs, with laughter and jokes high up on the menu. The wine flowed, the tongues wagged incessantly—Margaret's as hard as anyone else's. Of course, they always deferred to the Princess, calling her "Ma'am," and she accepted it as part of all that went with her Royal birth. But on her side, there was no standing on dignity. She could laugh as loudly as anyone, and was always ready with a wisecrack.

After dinner was finished and Margaret had lit her inevitable cigarette, the party would wander back again to the sitting room. Within minutes, the record-player went on. Brandy and cigars were ordered in quantity and the Margaret Set let their hair down, kicking off their shoes to dance on the carpets, helping themselves to drinks and sorting through the ¸incess's vast collection of records, from pop singers to Dixieland to real cool jazz. Incidentally, she had a very fine collection of classical music, too, but my Princess's taste was definitely low-brow, and for the most part, the symphonies, concertos and arias remained solidly in their covers. And it was to the accompaniment of foot-tapping music that the party continued. Once I went into the sitting room during one of these parties and there was Margaret, typically leading the group, jiving in her stockinged feet, her face flushed with excitement and one or two curls hanging over her forehead. I always felt that she could have carried on all night at any time—indeed this risk often seemed real as I waited, red-eyed, in the pantry for the signal to show the party off the premises!

Margaret was always there to see them off, still cracking jokes, still smoking out of her long cigarette holder, still looking lovely and lively. Regardless of the hour, she called out loudly, perhaps thanking them all for a wonderful evening. I stood next to her, silently watching them depart in their cars, through the main gate and out past the police lodge, each getting a salute from the weary policeman on duty.

These late nights were inevitably followed by the "morning after" which meant that Margaret would not be seen until the early afternoon. No such luck for me, of course. I was still expected to respond to the urgent calls of the Royal dogs and take them out for their early-morning exercise. But at least she showed signs of sympathy when I stifled a yawn.

But, in retrospect, it always seemed worth it to watch my Princess when she was ready to go out for a special evening. She absolutely loved putting on a new dress, making herself look her most radiant, and waiting for the guests to arrive. A new dress was a tonic to her and was enough to make her bubble over with high spirits and good humor. When she wore a dress with a flared skirt, she would not take the elevator to the ground floor, but would prefer to walk down the main stairs, holding her skirts up slightly and peering down as she trod the stairs, pausing momentarily to catch a glimpse of herself in the many mirrors flanking the staircase.

She was so full of excitement that she would open conversations with me about her dresses and ask me if I liked the one she was wearing.

I remember when she was expecting Billy Wallace to call and take her out. She had been in her bedroom for over an hour, dressing. I met her when she came downstairs again as she flounced along the main corridor. I followed her to the sitting room, where she beckoned me inside. I waited hesitantly inside the door and watched while she minced her way to the center of the room and did a few quick little dance steps, swirling her skirts in a pirouette.

She looked adorable, standing there in her beautiful deep blue evening gown flashing with sequins and pearls, wearing a diamond necklace and small diamond earrings and, on her left wrist, a gold watch. For a moment she stood there, with one toe of her openwork evening shoes peeping from beneath the hem of her skirt. Then she asked: "Do you like this new dress, John?" And she added: "I have only just got it."

I cocked my head to one side, as if giving great thought to the matter, before I replied: "Of course I do, Your Royal Highness. I think all your dresses are wonderful."

"Thank you very much," she said gravely. Then she turned, humming in her happiness, and walked over to the drink tray. "I want you to go to the door to meet Mr. Wallace." She glanced at her watch. "He will be here in a few moments."

"Yes, Ma'am," I said, and withdrew.

As usual, Billy Wallace was late. Fifteen minutes late. He arrived, however, quite unflustered in his tiny blue bubble car as always. For although he was able to travel in a chauffeur-driven Rolls-Royce any time he chose, he preferred to drive himself in the maneuverable little three-wheeler. It was to be the point of a very amusing incident involving Margaret a few weeks later, but I will save that episode for a later chapter.

I ushered in Mr. Wallace in the normal manner, bowing him into the main door and inviting him to follow me to the Princess's sitting room—although he knew the way blindfolded. When I tapped on the door and entered to announce Mr. Wallace, Margaret was posed on the settee, her wide skirts billowing up around her, smoking the inevitable cigarette. As soon as Billy entered, she dropped her holder into the ashtray and skipped across the floor. The two of them met about six paces from the door, and Margaret greeted him in the usual manner—that is, putting her hands on his and tip-toeing to kiss him on both cheeks. And she welcomed him with an affectionate "Hello, darling Billy. Do come in."

He replied, "Good evening, Ma'am," and gave a slight nod of the head. Margaret's three dogs joined in the welcome, snapping around his legs, and he bent to stroke them. At the same time, he struck up a conversation about something or other and they were off on another evening of high spirits.

That evening, they went to the London theatre and were back again at around two.

I have mentioned the dogs again in passing. Perhaps I ought to say that they did indeed spend all their time with the Princess in her room when she was at home. They always behaved themselves, and one hardly noticed they were there, but I like to recall with a chuckle the first time I ever heard them criticize the Princess. It was one afternoon when she had no engagements. I had gone up to the sitting room on one of my regular calls, and found the room empty. I puzzled for a moment whether I should wait for her, when I heard the faint strains of a piano. There was a huge grand piano in the drawing room and, on occasion, the Princess relaxed by playing it. She played very well. As I walked up the corridor towards the room, Margaret started to sing, accompanying herself expertly. I was enchanted to hear her cool soprano voice.

But I'm afraid that the dogs were not as receptive to Her

Royal Highness's performance. To my horror, they began whining plaintively. They grew louder and louder until their noise almost drowned poor Margaret's voice. Thinking that perhaps she would want them removed, I knocked and entered. But as I did so, Margaret broke off and burst into a fit of laughter, pointing helplessly at Roly, the King Charles spaniel.

"Look at him," she giggled. "He thinks he can sing as well as me. Don't you Roly?" And as she stroked him, still chuckling, she added: "And perhaps he can."

"Oh, I'm sure I would rather hear you than the dog, Your Royal Highness," I said, diplomatically. And my Princess turned back to the piano, struck up fortissimo and sang loudly to the dog. Not to be outdone, Roly whined back even more loudly, and as I left, the session broke up as the Princess chased the dogs about the room—all four of them thoroughly enjoying themselves.

These, then, are some of the things that happened during a normal day at Clarence House. No two days were quite the same, naturally, but there was a routine even if it was broken by the spontaneous incidents and conversations I have mentioned.

But there was one other big regular item on the time table which was to be a constant source of wonder and amusement to me the entire time I was at Clarence House.

It concerned the Crankpots—that's Margaret's description, not mine.

I learned, in the first few days of my duties with the Princess, when I was discovering my way around the house, that it was I who was to have first access to her mail. The morning's post was taken from the main gate into the office, where two attendants sorted it roughly into personal letters for the Queen Mother and the Princess and mail for the administrative side of the House. The letters for her Royal Highness was handed to me at breakfast time. And, as I have told, I had to take them into the sitting room for the Princess to read when she came downstairs.

And it was through my handling of the mail that I learned of her loathing for a certain section of the outside community who wrote to her daily, and for whom she reserved the special name "Crankpots."

These were the people who penned the begging letters,

setting out their endless tales of hard luck and misfortune, asking for an audience with her, and wanting her to assist them financially or to sort out their domestic problems. But worse than these were the letters—many of them from mental hospitals throughout the world—from demented men and women asking intimate questions about her personal life and hinting of the pleasures that they might afford her, were they given her permission to visit her in her apartments. On top of this, there were half a dozen quite serious letters offering proposals of marriage to my Princess from men claiming to be fabulously rich and offering her to keep her in wealth for the rest of her life.

Some of them wrote again and again, though they never got a reply. Nor did the Princess ever bother to take the matter to any of the Court officials who might have had the police investigate.

She was only concerned that she herself did not have to open any of them. I suppose that she must have done so quite frequently in earlier days, for she certainly knew such things existed. And perhaps the most loathsome of all were the packages addressed to her. She could easily be fooled by these, as they might well contain a gift from one of her friends, or a delivery of photographic equipment. On the other hand, they might come from a Crankpot. . . .

Shortly after I took over the job of sorting her mail, she came to me and spoke about these parcels. With bitterness and disgust in her voice, she told me: "John, on no account must you ever bring packages to me which have not been carefully checked beforehand. I want you to dispose of them and their contents if they seem in any way questionable to you."

I promised that I would do this, but I was a little mystified. It was less than a month before I learned the reason for her despair. A plain, brown-paper parcel arrived in the mail and, conscious of the warning I had been given, I took a chance and opened it. To my horror, I found that it contained a complete set of flimsy underwear, together with a disgustingly suggestive note from some anonymous wretch. I carried the parcel to the tiny courtyard at the rear of the house and threw it into the refuse bin and burned the note in the kitchen.

But the letters were an easier proposition to sort out. Every morning, after delivering breakfast to the Princess, I pulled a chair up to the table in the pantry and sorted through the pile of letters.

By the time I had finished, about seven or eight out of twenty or so letters would find their way to the Princess. So you can see that the ratio of genuine letters to the other kind was roughly two to one. That was what the Princess had to contend with. That is what it means to be an attractive young Princess in this strange world. It is an odd comment on our times that Margaret should have received literally hundreds of these weird communications a year—the price, I suppose, of being born into such a position. Or just an occupational hazard, as much a part of her life as the detectives who, unseen, watch over the Princess and all the other members of the Royal Family, wherever they are, twenty-four hours a day.

To help me weed out these objectionable letters, I established my own filing system. From one of the drawers allocated to me in the pantry, I took a folder containing old envelopes and postmarks torn from previous letters of a doubtful nature. Anything which I thought to be suspect, I checked against my file. Time and again, the telltale handwriting or some obscure postmark would reveal them. It is a commentary, perhaps, on the intelligence of some of the people who sent them that they never had the sense to change the place from which they posted their horrible writings.

But the letters which were genuine—from friends of the Princess—I recognized immediately. All her friends knew the code to adopt when writing to my Princess. It was so simple, but effective. After addressing the envelope, they wrote their initials discreetly and in small letters in the bottom left-hand corner of the envelope. I looked there first—to pick out the "W.W." which I knew was Billy Wallace, or the "D.E." for Dominic Elliott. Lord Plunkett wrote the plain, aristocratic "P" for his initials. Later on in my service, I became familiar with the initials "T.A.J."—they had me wondering, in those early days. . . .

The genuine letters I carried unopened to her sitting room.

Of course, letters were not the only means of communication open to the Crankpots. Some of them tried their luck on the telephone. Ten or a dozen times a week. Sometimes, I was called on my own telephone extension and asked if the Princess knew a Mr.——. I was the first refuge of the telephone operators who felt uncertain about these calls. Often they would come from as far away as America or Australia. It has happened that a telephone Crankpot has posed as a distant relative of the Royal Family and has had the cheek to say that he wished to speak only to the Princess on some urgent family matter.

A call such as this would turn the whole household upside down for a few minutes. Calls on other extensions were put through to the offices or to the Lady in Waiting, Miss Peake, to question the caller's identity. Anything rather than put it through to the sitting room in which the Princess sat, quite unaware of the panic.

Eventually, it would be decided that the caller was obviously a Crankpot and then he was told—either by the switchboard operator or perhaps even by the duty policeman on his extension at the main gate—that the Princess was not in residence, and that it would be advisable not to call again. If it proved to be a genuine call, the Princess took it wherever she happened to be. Like almost any other woman, she came into her own on the telephone, and loved nothing better than to stand, sit or lie down talking, talking, talking for anything up to half an hour.

But there was one Crankpot whom the Princess could tolerate. In fact, she had quite a soft spot for him. There is no doubt that he was classed as a Crankpot, but throughout my service with Margaret at Clarence House he sent her a bunch of flowers every Monday morning. The modest little posy was sent along from a West End florist by messenger boy. Attached to the bunch was a card, always written in the same hand, which said something quite simple and dignified, like: "With all my love and best wishes, E." They were always placed in her sitting room, displayed on their own along with some of the more expensive bouquets. Margaret liked to inspect the flowers as they were changed, and she always passed E's bunch without comment, until one morning something happened which underlined how fond she had grown of this harmless and charming gesture.

Up to that time, I had always thought that the flowers came from one of Margaret's personal friends, simply because he used an initial, as her friends did when they wrote to her.

Often enough, I tried to think who "E" could be. I ran through the list of titled people she knew. I thought it would be Lord Someone because of the single initial—but eventually I gave it up.

Then, one Monday morning when we had all just returned from Windsor, I was in the sitting room with Margaret, having answered her summons. She had been in the room, I judged, only a few minutes, after changing out of her traveling clothes. As I closed the door behind me, the Princess was stalking round the room looking at the flowers.

After a moment or two, she frowned. With her arm on her hip, she asked me mildly: "John, where are the flowers from my Crankpot friend?"

I stood there. After all, I did not at that moment, know who her Crankpot friend was. "I beg your pardon, Your Royal Highness?" I asked expectantly.

"My Crankpot. Where are his flowers?" There was a note of exasperation in her voice.

I looked around me while she stood waiting for an answer. I felt uncomfortable. I just didn't like being caught in a guessing game like this, especially when my Princess quite obviously expected me to have the answers. "Whom do you mean, Your Royal Highness?" I asked at last.

"Oh, come along, John. You must know who I mean. The one that signs himself E. Where are they?"

There was nothing I had in the way of explanation, so I told her: "I'm afraid they haven't arrived today, Ma'am."

"What do you mean, they haven't arrived?" Margaret stamped her foot in annoyance. "They always come on Monday."

I was helpless, but I volunteered the only answer I had ever arrived at to the puzzle of E. I had worked it out, entirely to my satisfaction that the flowers might have come from one of Margaret's circle of court women, Lady——. I told her so, and it dispersed my Princess's annoyance.

"Oh, no," she said. "Not at all. They come from a very good Crankpot friend, you know." And she laughed. "Go away now and see if you can trace them. I am perfectly certain they must have arrived."

Sure enough, they had arrived, as always. But as I had myself been at Windsor, the flowers had been unwrapped that morning by Mrs. Gordon, who had taken them to the

Princess's bedroom and put them in a small vase. It was there I found them, a small bunch of mimosa and narcissi.

With a ridiculous feeling of relief, I carried them downstairs again to the sitting room. When I showed them to her, Margaret was delighted. "I knew he wouldn't let me down," she said. "Bring them over here." And she trotted over to her desk, moving a much grander vase of blooms onto a table. "I'll have them right here today."

There were always plenty of flowers in the apartments at Clarence House. A great many of them were brought up by van a couple of times a week from the gardens of Windsor Castle. But even if they did come from within the Family, they were not sent to the Clarence House branch free of charge. In fact, the Queen's Household made a modest profit from their garden by selling them to the Queen Mother. They arrived usually on Mondays and Wednesdays, and very lovely they looked, but I'm afraid they rarely lasted more than a couple of days, even though I changed the water every twenty-four hours.

Another regular sale was the dozen fresh eggs, quart of milk and pat of freshly-made butter brought from the Castle to Clarence House each morning. It was just one of those little fads that people are entitled to, I suppose, but these items were used only by the Queen Mother and Margaret, and woe betide anyone who tried to pass them shop eggs or butter, or old milk.

This then, was life at Clarence House. You will have a fair picture of how things went day by day, and perhaps a better idea by now of the sort of person Margaret was. I hope you are glad to find that she is, indeed, a warm, human person who retained her independence within the fairly rigid demands of the Royal Family of Great Britain.

But now, I shall move on to some of the moving, hilarious, sad, and exciting things that happened to my Princess. Events in which I shared as the omnipresent, almost invisible being who was so accepted that Margaret could pass through a whole array of emotions just as if she were alone.

First I will tell you about one of the things which touched me deeply. I was not directly involved emotionally, but somehow it affected me a great deal, as a poignant scene in a film might fetch a lump to the throat.

I refer to the last meeting between Group Captain Peter

Townsend and Princess Margaret. It came quite unexpectedly for me and the rest of the world too, I think. It happened at Clarence House.

The Queen Mother, the Princess and the handsome Group Captain were there for the last goodby—and so was I.

Chapter Seven

Princess Margaret's love affair with the handsome Group Captain Peter Townsend—the romance which caught so strongly at the imagination of men and women the world over—had ended in 1955, crushed by the weight of duty to the Throne, that phrase which has been at once the strength and the weakness of the British Royal Family. Margaret herself had administered the death-blow to the hopes of practically everyone that she would finally marry Townsend, with her historic announcement that she would renounce the marriage. The love that had grown up between them from the time that Townsend was an equerry to the late King George VI and Margaret was a teenage Princess was officially ended with those few sentences. It was the first and last official announcement on the subject. Thereafter, Townsend went on a world tour and Margaret climbed slowly back to her former position as a leading member of the Royal Family, unencumbered with embarrassing rumors about her love for a commoner.

How curious that five years later, she should defy the rules and choose another commoner and this time marry him—and announce the fact with the same suddenness with which she had eclipsed the former.

In between these two events, Townsend had flitted briefly back into the picture at odd times, living on the Continent and making quick excursions to London—and bringing with him clouds of publicity. But it is to his last visit that I am now going to refer. That time in the summer of 1959 when not only did he come back to London, but was invited to tea at Clarence House.

That visit aroused endless curiosity. Hundreds of reporters, photographers and correspondents from the world's newspapers besieged Clarence House that afternoon when it was discovered he had been there. Hundreds more, ordinary Londoners this time, crowded around the Mall and St. James's hoping, perhaps, for another glimpse of the man they had read about so often, and hoping that this event perhaps would lead to the resurrection of the Margaret-Townsend love affair which they had taken so dearly to their hearts.

Of course, it didn't. As I well know, for I saw it, that meeting was their last goodby. It was the last kiss between people who had finally accepted their fates, had made their peace with each other and were preparing to go their separate ways forever.

The whole visit was totally unexpected to myself and the other members of the Clarence House staff. Indeed, many of the other staff did not realize he was in the House until half an hour after his arrival. Until the early afternoon, it had been a normal day. But after lunch, the Princess called me to the sitting room and told me—her face radiant and beautiful—"John, I am expecting a very special guest to take tea with me this afternoon. Lay three places in here because Her Majesty Queen Elizabeth"—even at this time, she used the formal mode of address with which she always referred to her mother—"will be taking tea with us." I nodded, a little baffled by this depature from the normal, and asked what time I should expect the "special guest."

Margaret looked at her watch, quite plainly bursting with impatience, like a child about to be taken on a seaside treat, and said: "Four-thirty . . . and John, do be there on time. My guest will not be late."

During the afternoon, not realizing that I was preparing the stage for one of the most poignant moments in the life of my Princess, I laid out the card table in the center of the sitting room and pulled up three chairs ready for tea to be served. I spread a pale blue tablecloth over the green baize table top, and about 4 o'clock, I carried in the tea things. I remember they used the white china tea service with pale blue edging around the lips of the cups. Finally, I fetched three pale blue table napkins and a plate of tiny sandwiches and a cakestand with a selection of little cakes. In the pantry, I saw to the preparation of a pot of the Princess's favorite China tea.

It was 4:25. All was ready. . . .

With a final quick brush of my uniform, I straightened my tie and walked down to the main door and took up my waiting position, still not knowing whom to expect. At exactly 4:30, just as the Princess had forecast, the wooden gates of Clarence House swung open and into the drive glided a green chauffeur-driven saloon car. It swept across the courtyard and halted a few paces from the front step. When it stopped, I was ready, and stepped forward to open the rear nearside door. To my utter astonishment, I recognized the suntanned figure of the passenger as that of Peter Townsend. I had become quite used to meeting the famous, but this time I know I hesitated while a thousand thoughts flashed through my mind. But it could not have lasted more than a second, for Townsend climbed without comment out of his seat and pulled himself up to his full height on the stone-flagged ground beside me. I waited a moment or two after closing the car door, while Townsend tugged at his rather crumpled jacket and adjusted the knot of his maroon tie. He wore a dark blue suit, which I judged had seen a good deal of service.

As I stood for those few seconds, I stared at him partly to catch his eye, partly out of pure surprise. I can recall so very clearly the look of slight apprehension on his face, clouding the firm, almost pugnacious set of his jaw. It seemed to me in retrospect that he had almost had to steel himself for this visit, although at that time, of course, I had not the slightest notion of what was to happen, or what the purpose of the call was going to be. But as we stood there, I did not have time to speculate. Townsend slid back the sleeve of his jacket for a quick glance at his watch, then started toward the door, looking across to me for the first time.

I bowed my head slightly as he spoke. "Good afternoon," he said in his soft, pleasant voice and I replied: "Good afternoon, sir. Will you please follow me? Her Royal Highness and Her Majesty are expecting you."

He waited while I walked past him to lead the way out of the brilliant sunshine of that summer's day, into the porch and the cool of the main corridor. At this point, Townsend's eagerness to be in got the better of him. He sprang lightly up the three carpeted stairs and was past me as we turned the corner into the passage leading down to Margaret's room.

There, I got my next surprise. For, in complete abandonment of the usual Royal rules, both the Princess and the Queen Mother had left the room and were walking along the corridor toward us. Never before, or since, did I know any of the Royals do anything but wait in their rooms for the guest to be brought to them. It was an expression of how welcome Townsend was and had been at Clarence House, not only to the woman he loved, but to her mother too. I guessed that the Royal couple had heard the car draw up, for they were halfway down the corridor, their faces smiling with anticipation.

Townsend lifted his head and his eyes locked on Margaret. I was quite forgotten in this heart-touching scene for, never taking her eyes from him, Margaret dashed away from the mildly restraining hand of her mother and ran to meet Townsend. She stopped two feet from him, looking up at him. They searched each other's faces for a fraction of a second, then both took a pace forward and embraced. Margaret reached up and put her delicate white hands on his shoulders and kissed him firmly, full on the lips. They lingered over this kiss, neither wanting to draw back, it seemed. I noticed Margaret had slipped out of the heels of her shoes as she tip-toed up to meet the tall Townsend. At last, they parted and Margaret leaned back, taking his hands but keeping them still on her waist. Only then, for the first time that afternoon, did she speak.

"Oh Peter . . ." was all she said. And I was close enough to hear the sigh in her voice and see the liquid sparkle in her eyes. Then: "It's wonderful to see you again."

She wore a shiny dark blue satin dress and her full skirt was crushed against him. Then, as she backed away slightly, her hands went unconsciously to her dress, smoothing the skirt straight again. I never saw two people so lost in the magic of a moment like that. It lasted less than a minute, I suppose, though it seemed a golden age to me at the time. Only when they parted did it occur to me that throughout, the Queen Mother had been standing watching three paces away, having walked quietly after her daughter. In her understandable excitement, Margaret had broken another of the rules—that of Royal precedence. By the book, the Queen Mother should have been the first to greet their guest because she was the senior member of the household, but it was quite obvious that she too was happy to throw the book to the winds and allow Margaret to welcome Townsend in her most unusual, most un-Royal, but most whole-hearted way.

As Margaret and Townsend parted, she smiled fondly, glancing both at the tall Group Captain and at her daughter as she did so. She stepped past Margaret, who, with a little bow toward her mother and a last smile at his face, looked over her shoulder and stepped back a pace or two beside me.

The Queen Mother held Peter Townsend's hand for a few moments in silent welcome to the man who so very nearly became her own son-in-law. "Good afternoon, Peter, it's been a very long time." She paused and, with a firm shake of Townsend's hand, added: "It's so very lovely to have you here again." At that moment, her pleasure so obviously displayed, I wondered whether that gracious lady ever regretted the force of Royal duty and the pressure which had been brought to bear on Margaret by the advisers to the Throne to issue the edict which finally slammed the door on Townsend. Now he stood before her, and with an almost imperceptible bow, answered: "Ma'am, I am more than thrilled to be back here. More so to be here meeting yourself and Princess Margaret than simply to be back in my own London again."

Up until this moment, I had been an unnoticed observer, and the three had seemed oblivious of me. It was the Queen Mother who broke the magic spell for me. She released Townsend's hand and looked at me, half in surprise. With a warm smile, she said simply: "I'm sure tea is quite ready now." I understood. I replied: "Yes, Your Majesty," and I moved past the group, bowing as I did so. I walked slightly ahead of Margaret and Townsend, and the Queen Mother brought up the rear as I led the way to the sitting room. I opened the door, and stood back a pace or two outside in the corridor. The couple stood aside to allow the Queen Mother to enter the room first. She looked the picture of regality as she passed me, her straight-skirted rust satin afternoon dress worn with a silver grey fox fur hanging loosely over her shoulder.

Margaret passed me next and, with her mother's back to her, she permitted herself an affectionate glance over her shoulder to Townsend. He smiled fondly in return, but no words were spoken. No one said anything more while I watched them move into the room. The Queen Mother turned and looked at Townsend again, a smile on her lips and a serious look in her eyes. They formed a semi-circle and Townsend began to speak as I slowly closed the door and walked thoughtfully back down the corridor.

In the pantry I found out that all the other servants had been dismissed from the front part of the house shortly before Townsend arrived. I sat alone for a while musing on the scenes I had been privileged to witness. I felt sure —and rightly as it turned out—that the real significance of this visit was that Margaret had decided to take the opportunity to say her final goodby to Townsend before any other romance, this time of a permanent nature, prevented her from so doing. I smoked a couple of cigarettes as I pondered. One or two of the servants came in to ask if it really was Townsend upstairs. Like me, they were accustomed to seeing the top people in and around Clarence House and elsewhere in the Royal houses, but found their blasé attitude demolished by the intriguing tea party.

Half an hour passed quickly. And at about 5 o'clock my musings and guarded comments to the other servants were interrupted by the buzzing of the call indicator on the wall of the pantry. I looked up. It showed: "H.R.H. Sitting Room." I stubbed out my half-smoked cigarette, gave myself the customary brush down and left. The house was quite silent as I walked through the corridors. I found myself feeling nervously excited—the sort of feeling I had when I met my Princess for the very first time. I reached the sitting room and paused for a deep breath before opening the door. In the sunlight which flooded through the windows, I found the three just rising from the table. Townsend was facing me. The Princess had been sitting to his left, the Queen Mother to his right. Their soft chatter stopped as I opened the door. I entered and stood at attention just inside the room. "You rang, Your Majesty?" I said, feeling at that moment like a film extra rehearsing a rather corny scene in a sumptuous musical comedy. And the Queen Mother replied: "Yes, John, our guest is ready to leave." They never mentioned his name to me. I bowed again and stood on the threshold. They walked round the table, the Queen Mother leading the way from the room. I stepped aside as she left. Behind her, Margaret and Peter Townsend walked slowly, almost reluctantly, out of the room—this time hand in hand. Once more, she was looking up at him, smiling. But there was a serious expression on her face and on his as he steadily returned her gaze. Disregarding anyone or anything, they passed me in step and turned for their last walk together down the passage that led to the main corridor and the door. As they passed, I smelled the exquisite perfume that Margaret had used ... something extra special, perhaps, I speculated.

Outside the room, the Queen Mother paused and they formed a group of three again as I brushed past them to lead the way to the door. I walked ahead of them to the door, opened it a little and peeped out. In the drive, Townsend's car was already drawn up, the chauffeur sitting stolidly at the wheel staring idly ahead. At the main gate, the duty policeman waited, looking over at the door, waiting for it to open—his signal to open the big front gate. I closed the door again, feeling that this moment needed all the privacy of a confessional. There was no one else in the corridor except Margaret, Townsend, the Queen Mother and myself.

They stood now at the top of the three stairs, silent still, about to say their goodby. I waited with my hand on the brass doorknob, trying to be still lest any movement of mine disturb them. They had stopped in a semi-circle, the Queen Mother at the center, Townsend to her left. It was as if they were waiting for someone to take a photograph, they were so still. Then, with an audible sigh, Peter Townsend turned away from the Princess to her mother and taking her right hand in both of his, bent to kiss her gently on both cheeks. The Queen Mother nodded, as if some unspoken message had passed between them. Then he spoke, in a voice which wavered ever so slightly with the emotion of the moment, and in little more than a whisper said: "Your Majesty, I ... I am so happy to have seen you again, yet so sorry to be leaving you."

She did not reply. The words, no doubt, had been said

over the card table in the sitting room. With a half-glance at Margaret, standing tensely at her other side, she stepped back. I watched, and I admit I felt the sting of tears in my eyes and the lump in my throat which comes at such moments. I am not ashamed to say that I have rarely been so moved, so afflicted by the sadness of others as I was on that day, that hot day at the unromantic hour of teatime.

As the Queen Mother withdrew a few paces—yet I felt she might have disappeared for the next few minutes—Townsend squarely faced my Princess. They gazed into each other's eyes, searching, it seemed, for words that even at this moment could never been spoken. He took Margaret by the hand, bent down from his six feet two inches and kissed her lovingly on both cheeks.

He seemed overcome. He frowned and seemed unable to put into words the feeling that must have been pounding inside him. All those years that they had known each other, talked together, fallen in love, perhaps made plans which they believed in, and the heartache of their parting must have crossed his mind at that moment. And now he was parting from Princess Margaret once more. This time for good.

As Peter Townsend kissed Margaret, I caught sight of the Queen Mother. She was watching them, a gentle look in her eyes. Then, at the moment of their kiss, she turned away. It was a truly majestic move, signifying that she approved and wished the star-crossed couple to embrace without the restraint of her stare. I, too, lowered my eyes and stood as impassively as I knew a Royal servant must. Yet I shall always remember Margaret best as I saw her in that moment. No matter how often I now see her in photographs and in the newsreels, no matter with whom I see her, I shall never forget those precious moments when Margaret had forgotton Royalty and was simply an unhappy woman parting from the man for whom she had felt all the emotions that love can bring.

As they embraced, her eyes were closed. Her chin, held high and proudly, trembled ever so slightly. I knew she was near to tears and I could almost feel the fight she was putting up to prevent them from filling her eyes. I suppose only a woman with Margaret's strict Royal training could have held on to herself at that time. Reluctantly, she allowed Townsend to pull himself away from her and take his hand from hers. This was the moment of parting. Still no words had been spoken between them, but this was their last goodby. That kiss had said more than a volume for them both.

I did not need to be told. I opened the big doors and let the sun stream in. It was like switching on the light in a darkened room. Everything came to life again. The tenderness was banished with Townsend's decisive step toward the door. Without a further glance at the Queen Mother, he dragged his gaze from Margaret, straightened his shoulders and turned on his heel. He strode out into the courtyard without a backward glance and allowed me to open the door of his car. I stood aside as he threw himself into the back seat, staring painfully ahead, refusing to look back. As I bent to shut the door, his eyes met mine and I read a chapter of despair in his look.

Now, his eyes flashed to the doorway where Margaret and the Queen Mother were standing side by side to watch him drive away. Above them, the windows along the side of Clarence House were dotted with the faces of servants, looking eagerly down into the driveway, straining for a glimpse of the famous visitor. And so the magic of the moment of farewell was lost. I felt I wanted to get the whole thing over, to urge Townsend to go, to shut the doors of Clarence House on the rest of the world and to allow my Princess to be alone with her thoughts.

The motor of Townsend's car purred as the chauffeur prepared to drive away. I stepped back from the car, so as not to interrupt the line of sight between Townsend and the two women standing in the porch. The Queen Mother was standing quite still, smiling steadily. Then she turned and looked straight at Margaret who stood ashen-faced, her gaze still fixed on the man in the car. The Princess flashed a last smile and with her right hand, she gave a sort of helpless wave at shoulder height, dropped her hand, and then she too turned, to look at her mother as if seeking help to see her through some agonizing crisis. Now, as one, they looked again at Townsend for the last time. Without even waiting for the car to move off, they turned and walked side by side, their heads held high, into the House, up the steps and were lost to my view as they turned into the passage to the sitting room.

Through the rear door window of the car, I saw Peter Townsend's lips move as he gave the driver some instruction and instantly, the car was moving. Its tires crunched softly on the pathway. I waited, my hands clasped behind my back, while the car completed the turn in the drive and swept down again toward the main gate. Through the back window, I could see the top of Townsend's head. He was leaning against the back cushions of the seat, apparently staring straight ahead. As they passed through the gates, the policeman on duty saluted gravely and I saw Townsend's hand raise in acknowledgement and continue upwards to stroke his hair, a nervous movement which was a habit of his. Now the car was gone, nosing its way past the guards, through the crowds which had gathered in the street outside. I watched the back of that light-haired head until the last moment. It turned neither to left nor right, but—a second before Townsend vanished—his shoulders dropped and he appeared to slump down in his seat. The crowd outside made little noise. There was none of the cheering, the cries of "good luck," which were the normal accolade.

It seemed they sensed the mood of the man. And indeed, there could be no mistaking the air of despair which surrounded the lonely figure being driven away from his last contact with the woman he so very nearly had married. After he disappeared, there came the sympathetic murmurings of the crowd waiting across the courtyard as they broke up. They were drawing their own conclusions from their brief glimpse of Townsend. The policeman on the gate closed it with a rattle and retreated again to his box. Filled with the sadness which was everywhere in the air despite the bright sunshine, I stood rooted to the spot for a few more moments. I had not moved since Townsend had got into his car, and now I walked slowly into Clarence House and shut the doors. The corridor was deserted and there was silence, a brooding purple silence everywhere.

Margaret and the Queen Mother had already disappeared into the Princess's sitting room. When I reached the end of the corridor, I found the door already shut and inside was quite still. I hesitated outside the door. In any other circumstances, my next job would have been to go in and clear away the dirty tea things, but this time was different. To hell with the teacups, I thought. To intrude at such a moment would be ghastly. And I left as quietly as I had come.

I went up to my room and threw myself down on my little bed. It was ridiculous, I reasoned with myself, to feel so miserable at something which really had nothing to do with me. But had it nothing to do with me? For the first time, I examined my thoughts and feelings about the relationship between Margaret and her personal footman. I was a servant and she a Princess, yet I saw her every day, in all sorts of situations and moods and, like it or not, I found I had become emotionally bound up with my Princess. That day there was no escape from my enforced sharing of her sadness. With this realization, I got up and went down again to the pantry. I busied myself for half an hour, evaded the questions of the other servants until at about six. The indicator buzzed, calling me to Margaret's room again.

It was exactly as it had been, the tea things still lying in disarray over the card table, an ashtray nearby with two or three stubs in it, a cake neatly cut in two and left, a cup half full of weak tea, now quite cold. Margaret was sitting at her desk, writing. When I drew near her, I saw that three-quarters of a page of her personal diary was filled with her neat handwriting. . . .

At my approach, she stopped writing but barely looked up. Over her shoulder she said quietly: "I shall be dining with Her Majesty tonight."

That was all. And she looked down again at the words she had written. I replied: "Yes, Your Royal Highness," and walked over to the card table. It was most unusual for the Princess to join her mother for dinner in the evening, but I was past surprise at the events of the day. Automatically my mind counted through the arrangements necessary for the dinner in the first floor sitting room where the Queen Mother spent her day. As quickly and as carefully as I could, I gathered the tea thing onto a tray and left the room. When I turned to close the door behind me, Margaret was writing once more in her diary.

That evening, I waited on the table shared by Margaret and the Queen Mother. One of the Queen Mother's footmen

helped. The two women sat at a round table placed beneath the chandelier which remained unlit. Only the soft
glow of the wall lights illuminated the sitting room and only
the clink of cutlery on china broke the silence. . . .

They sat facing each other, both deep in their own
thoughts, not caring too much for the food. The Queen
Mother did manage to eat the simple three-course meal, but
Margaret sat picking with her fork. She ate in the American
style, using her fork in her right hand. Both women were still
wearing their afternoon dresses, a most unusual departure
from the normal, for both usually insisted on changing into
something a little more suited to the evening, despite the
fact that they might have only themselves to please.

The only remarks which interrupted the meal were my
inquiries as to their needs and the occasional refusal from
Margaret. One could even hear the odd creak of a chair and
the muffled pad of my footsteps on the carpet. When I
scraped a spoon over a silver salver, it sounded like thunder.
That meal remains quite the strangest I ever saw. It was
almost eerie. And the absence of Margaret's usual mealtime
chatter was depressing.

The meal took a good hour to consume, partly because,
to our surprise, both footmen were dismissed from the
room altogether after serving each course and we had to
listen outside and judge whether they had finished and would
require us again. I remember I found the other footman and
myself were somehow affected by the heavy silence from
inside the sitting room.

But eventually, they finished the meal. As always, Margaret fitted a cigarette into her holder and lit it with her
lighter. She blew a cloud of smoke into the air, and she
and her mother rose from the table and went across to the
settee drawn up adjacent to the electric heater. It had
been turned on in the chill of the approaching night and at
first, they both sat down side by side on the settee. But as we
cleared away the table, they both stood up again as if
searching for something to do. Margaret stubbed out her
cigarette three-quarters unsmoked and immediately slotted
another into her holder with a kind of nervously concentrated air. Having lit it, she stood with one arm behind her
back, staring into the red glow of the heater.

The Queen Mother walked away from her, across to her

desk and rummaged on it for a moment before finding her spectacles. Incidentally, few people are aware that the Queen Mother has to wear glasses for reading. She wears them only in the confines of her sitting room and never in public, even when reading official speeches, which are always written in large type to prevent her embarrassment.

She held the glasses to her eyes and picked up the evening papers which had been laid, as always, on her desk. She had the latest editions, for I was able to see from the center of the room, that they had splashed the afternoon news in large letters across the front page.

One said simply: "Townsend Goes to Tea."

The Queen Mother stood with her back to Margaret while she scanned the headlines of each of the three papers in turn. It was about 9:30 when the other footman and I finished clearing away the table. I had just picked it up to carry outside when Margaret spoke for the first time.

Without further preamble of any kind, she simply called across the room: "Goodnight, Mother." I had gone outside the door by this time. Through the closed door, as I prepared to dismantle the table upon which the couple had been eating, I heard a murmured exchange between Margaret and her mother. Then the door opened and out strode Margaret, her face set. Ignoring me, she walked across the corridor to where the elevator was waiting with the doors open. Quite expressionless, she turned to face the open door, lifted her hand to the button and the doors slid shut. I did not know whether she went up to her bedroom or down to the sitting room, for I was busy now with my own chores.

It must have been half an hour later that I finished in the pantry and thought about retiring for the night. I decided that I had better take a look at Margaret's sitting room for a last time, lest there were any messages, or something that needed clearing away before the morning. At any rate, I went up. However, as I drew near, I heard music coming from the sitting room—classical music. The melody, slow, soft and caressing, wafted through the closed door. And for the second time that day, I hesitated to intrude upon my Princess.

The fact that she was playing classical music at all was enough to demonstrate her state of mind. She had a magni-

ficent collection of records, but although she numbered many
classics among them, she rarely played these.

Thoroughly worn out by the emotions I had seen in
others and felt in myself that day, I returned to the pantry
and looked around for some other job to pass the time.
There was none, so I made myself comfortable as I could in
a chair at the table and lit a cigarette. I found an evening
paper which had splashed the Townsend visit in big headlines. I read it and shook my head. The paper had written
a column on the visit, but on examination it said nothing,
for no one could know, as I knew what had happened, or
how, or why. I smoked and read until a little after eleven.
I looked at my watch and rose, I made up my mind to
take another look—or listen—for Margaret. I walked up to
the sitting room and this time the door was open and the
room stood in darkness. I crossed the threshold and switched
on the light and took a look round the deserted room.

The air was heavy with cigarette smoke and on the side
table by the settee, an ashtray contained a cigarette end
which still smoldered a little, indicating that the Princess
had left the room but a few moments before. On Margaret's
desk was an empty glass. I picked it up and it left a little
ring of wet on the desk top. The glass had contained whisky.
Next to it was an ashtray with half a dozen cigarette stubs
crushed in it.

Then it caught my eye. Lying openly on the desk was that
secret, personal thing which Margaret treasured. Her diary.
What had she written against that day, I wondered? I stood
in the soft lighting, Margaret's empty glass in my hand and
stared down at the book for what must have been two or
three minutes. I knew temptation then, for it would have
been simple to have opened the diary and read it. But I
could not even have touched the outer cover. I felt it would
be a sacrilege. Here was Margaret's mind, I suspected; all
her thoughts set down in her own meticulous handwriting.
Perhaps she had felt better about everything when she had
finished. Perhaps she would never even read it again. I
shrugged and turned away from the desk and poured myself
a drink in another glass and drained it in one gulp. I needed
it, and I raised my eyes to the ceiling to where, through
the bricks and mortar, Margaret would be sleeping. I had

the impression that Margaret would not have minded and would have understood my need for that drink.

I doubted if she was in fact asleep yet. The tension in her mind would need time to relax—that tension which had caused her to overlook her most careful protection of her diary, for instance. Throughout my life with Princess Margaret, she had kept that diary locked away in a drawer of her desk and slipped the key into one of her own hiding places. Every day, except this. . . .

Taking the drinks tray and the ashtrays, I crossed the room again and stood by the door. My hand on the light switch, I paused before I snapped off the light and ended one of the most intriguing events of my life. Then I snapped the switch off and closed the door.

The drama for which I had set the scene earlier had been played out. Now the curtain was down. . . .

Within ten minutes, I was in my own room, the dogs settled down and I lay in the darkness.

Drowsily, I let my thoughts wander over the day. Then I thought of the three photographs which stood continually on the small bedside table where Margaret lay.

They were snaps of Peter Townsend.

They remained there throughout my service at Clarence House. Not even when her romance with Antony Armstrong-Jones was sweeping away all the old cares, did Margaret have them taken away. Was she now, I wondered, lying awake looking at them? I recalled them to my mind easily, for I had seen them so often. The center picture showed Townsend looking sternly into the camera—whether the camera was held by Margaret herself, I never knew. The other two snaps were of opposite profiles of Townsend.

And so that day ended, and with it, the last of the stories of Peter Townsend's romance with my Princess. Only once after that did his name crop up during my service with the Princess. It was on the day of the announcement of his engagement to the lovely Belgian girl Marie Luce—who, to me, bore a startling resemblance to Margaret. And by then, Margaret was quite her old self, having apparently forgotten that day of sorrow. This time, the sight of the stark announcement, showing that Townsend had indeed made his future in a different direction, only aroused her to a brief flare of Royal anger—or was it bitterness?

I was the first to see the news. It happened on another sunny day when I had gone to the police lodge at the main gate to collect the evening newspapers. I had nothing particular on my mind and the duty policeman, whom I had come to know well by now and who usually detained me with some chit-chat or other, had not mentioned there was anything of special interest in the papers. It was while I was walking back, glancing at the papers, that it hit me.

The small paragraph in the stop press, with its large head-line, stopped me dead in my tracks. It read simply: "Townsend to Marry." My heart skipped a beat. How forcefully I remembered the last time that Townsend had come into Margaret's life and it seemed to me that the reading of this announcement could only bring her further distress.

My first thought was to keep the papers from Margaret altogether, but even as I plotted to do so, I realized that the story would be in the papers next morning, on the radio and on TV—and that even if she did not hear or see it herself, it was bound to be a subject of conversation which she would eventually pick up. So, with the hope that the engagement would not upset her, I folded the paper under my arm and walked resolutely towards the House.

I went straight to the sitting room and found my Princess writing letters at her desk with her back to the door. In reply to my knock, she had half-turned in her chair and as I entered, I had hoped simply to leave the papers without any ado, but it was just my luck that Margaret had to be in a perky mood—brought on no doubt by the fact that she had an engagement that evening with one of her escorts, the affable Billy Wallace.

"What is it, John?" she asked.

"The evening papers, Ma'am," I replied.

"Oh, put them on the desk, will you," and she motioned with her pen to lay them at her right side and carried on with her writing. As I put them down, she said "Thank you," rather absently, for she was concentrating on the letter before her. Purely by chance, it happened that I laid the papers down so that the stop press of one of them was uppermost and there for Margaret to see at a glance was the bold black headline: "Townsend to Marry."

It was quite usual at this time of the day for me to tidy up the room while Margaret sat at her desk, so I started on the flowers, putting them straight in their vases, emptying the ashtrays and putting the settee cushions to rights. I wanted to see how she would react to the announcement. I make no excuse for this, save that I had shared with her the anguish of the previous experience with Townsend.

The Princess continued writing while I started to straighten up the room. She stopped then, and stared at the wall, possibly staring into space while searching for words. Then she glanced down at the paper. I watched her, fascinated, as she put down her pen, picked up the paper and leaned back in her chair. She was reading the stop press.

She had her back to me, and she sat quite still. I was standing near the fireplace at the time and I looked around me in desperation for something which I might be doing should the Princess suddenly turn round. I had the premonition that something violent was going to happen. But not yet, apparently, for Margaret calmly laid the paper down on the desk once more and picked up her pen. I inwardly sighed with relief. There was to be no reaction, no show of emotion. . . .

Then it happened. With a suddenness which almost caused me to drop the ashtray I had picked up, Margaret flared into action. In one swift movement, she grabbed the paper with her left hand and hurled it with all her force across the room. It fluttered in the air and skidded on a side table in the corner of the room, still folded, curiously enough, and with the stark announcement still uppermost.

Once again, I was rooted to the spot, expecting this time a tirade from my Princess. Moments passed, with the atmosphere charged with tension and Margaret sitting bolt upright in her chair staring ahead of her.

Then she picked up her pen again and started writing as if nothing had happened. She seemed unaware that I was even there and I moved as quietly as I knew toward the door. As I went out, I looked back at the small figure at the desk on the far side of the room, and had the same dark feeling that had visited me when Townsend had called at Clarence House. I tip-toed out and shut the door softly behind me. Only then, to my surprise, did I find myself trembling slightly and sweating profusely inside my uniform.

Once again, I felt the curious unreality of sharing the emotions of someone who was, or should have been, nothing to me as a person but merely my employer. But I suppose, and indeed, I now know, that it is impossible to share a part of someone's life so closely without becoming emotionally involved with their feelings, their problems and their character. And, I realized, like it or not, I had come not only to understand but to sympathize deeply with the beautiful, human little figure I left sitting alone in that room.

Almost immediately, it was time to serve the Princess her tea in her room. She took it alone as usual and was still at her desk when I carried up the tray for her. I set it out near the desk and as I did so, she smiled over to me, a weary, resigned sort of smile, and said: "Thank you, John. Please don't wait."

It must have been half an hour later, shortly after 5:30 that I went back to the room. Now Margaret, wearing her low-cut pink and white afternoon dress with white shoes, was slumped on the settee, smoking and staring into the fire with a blank look on her face that seemed to say: "Well, that's that." The tea things had barely been touched, I noticed, except for one cup of tea. Margaret did not speak at all while I was in the room and I made my exit as quickly as I could.

Shortly after six, I was summoned back to the room. Her mood had changed. It was as if, in changing her afternoon dress for a gay, orange-colored tulip-style cocktail dress, and a pair of gold strap shoes, she had cast off her previous numbness. Now she was smiling as she spoke.

"John, I want you to take this up to Her Majesty Queen Elizabeth," she said, handing me a white envelope. I took it, noticing the usual signature in the bottom lefthand corner—just a plain "M."

"Yes, Your Royal Highness. Will there be anything more?" I asked, thinking that perhaps she might want a reply fetched down. "No, nothing," said Margaret, smiling again. "Off you go."

I carried the message up the stairs to the first floor sitting room and knocked. With permission, I entered the room to find the Queen Mother sitting reading a book in front of the fire. I handed her the note, which she inspected a moment, then I withdrew. I could guess the content of the note. It would draw the attention of the Queen Mother to the press announcement about Townsend. And there would be no reply.

I had a little less than an hour to kill now, before the arrival of the Princess's escort. She had warned me earlier in the day that a guest was expected.

I made myself some tea and waited until 7 p.m. when I went up to the front door and took a seat on one of the chairs just inside the door, my ear cocked for the arrival of the guest. Ten to fifteen minutes later Billy Wallace arrived, late as usual, in his little bubble car. He bounded from the vehicle looking spruce and debonair in his evening dress. I ushered him along to Margaret's sitting room and opened the door for him.

Margaret, who had been sitting on the settee, jumped to her feet when she saw him and hurried across the room.

Taking his hand fondly, she smiled: "Hello, darling Billy. Come in, I've been waiting for you."

"Good evening, Ma'am," came the formal answer. In my presence, I never heard him call her anything else but by this formal address.

All Margaret's former fury and sadness had gone. Here was the real Margaret, the lovely young woman, fresh and bubbling over with gaiety and happiness. Now she leaned up to kiss Billy Wallace lightly on the cheek and stood back holding his hand, almost hopping with excitement. I left them standing like that in the doorway and returned to my seat at the main entrance in readiness for their departure.

I risked a cigarette—strictly not allowed when on duty like this—but it was more than twenty minutes before I heard the sitting-room door slam and seconds later, saw the couple walk arm in arm into the corridor and toward me. Billy Wallace was talking and gesticulating with his free hand and had Margaret's rapt and amused attention. I though to myself that an evening out with him, with all the gaiety it promised, was the very thing that Margaret must have wished for most. It would be an evening in a club in London's West End, or a theatre, or both. As they passed me, Mr. Wallace put his hand under Margaret's arm and helped her lightly down the steps and out onto the driveway. In this manner, they walked across to Wallace's pale blue bubble car.

It looked ridiculous standing there, in place of the huge black Rolls-Royce which was Margaret's official carriage.

The complete aplomb with which Billy Wallace ushered Margaret into this tiny vehicle never ceased to amuse me. It certainly was not made for Royal etiquette, For one thing, since it had a left-hand drive, it was necessary for the driver to clamber in before the passenger. But Margaret waited patiently while Billy hauled himself into the driving seat first, to avoid having to climb over her had she been first in. He held open the hinged front for her, and Margaret, with an amused grin, stepped into the bubble with all the dignity and grace with which she might have stepped into her own limousine.

Then, with a wheezy groan, the car started and made off slowly down the drive. But not down to the main gate. On these informal outings, Margaret's escorts never drove out of the main gate. They always went round the front of the House and out through the tradesmen's entrance through the courtyard. This was a ruse—I believe originally planned by Margaret herself—to escape the crowds which were invariably waiting outside the House at any time of the day or evening. It wasn't that Margaret disliked them, but simply that she liked to be able to lead some part of her life away from the continual community stare.

I waited up until midnight before retiring, but they had not returned. The next morning, when I got up and walked out to the main gate lodge, the police who had been on duty throughout the night, smiled as he handed me the morning papers.

"Your little lady was late this morning," he volunteered.

"Oh, what time was it?" I asked.

He consulted his logbook for a second, then said: "4 o'clock, it was."

Later, as I had expected, I received the evidence that the Princess had had a late night. She did not get up until nearly 1 o'clock in the afternoon, looking a little worn, but happy.

Chapter Eight

At this time in my service with Her Royal Highness, such nights as this with Billy Wallace were to become the normal thing. As if throwing off the effects of her last contacts with Peter Townsend, she gave herself up to a whirl of parties, evenings at the theatre, night clubs and social engagements. Everywhere there was a big gathering of the cream of Britain's society, there was Margaret.

Practically every night, one of her escorts—they were given the title of the Margaret Set—drove up to Clarence House by car and taxi to whisk her away to another night out on the town. For her to return before midnight was unusual and I was very often in bed by the time she got back, driven to the house by her escort or perhaps a party of friends they had picked up during the evening.

These days, Margaret quite often took off for her evening at about 8 o'clock and I saw and heard no more of her until I went down to the main gate to fetch the papers in the morning. There might be a paragraph or a picture in the paper to tell where she had been the previous night. She could rarely escape the press entirely. Not unnaturally, they regarded her every movement as news and they tracked her comings and goings almost relentlessly.

I suppose it was just the price which is paid for Royal birth, but I have been with the Princess when she was traveling from London by rail or air, and the press photographers have practically stood on their heads for nothing more than a picture of Margaret walking along a railway platform. I know that Margaret thoroughly disliked some of the scuffles and turmoil which followed the general scramble for positions by the photographers, but she never allowed her inner feelings to get the better of her public face and never was she caught in anything but a warm, smiling and apparently quite happy frame of mind. But, on the Royal train for instance, I have seen her smile fade into a look of weary relief at having successfully run the gamut of the cameras.

If it were not through the morning papers that I caught up with Margaret's movements, there was always the duty policemen on the main gate. Every movement made by Margaret in and out of Clarence House was carefully noted down in their log book and they used to delight in telling me how the Princess had swept into the drive at two, three or even four in the morning. To those policemen, Margaret was always "your little lady" when they talked about her to me.

It only happened once that my Princess had not returned at all, even when I went down to collect the papers. But she came in just as I got there. While chatting to the police, I heard an all-too-familiar "Peep-peep" from outside the gate. My policeman friend looked at me for a moment, hurriedly buttoned up his tunic and sprang to the gate. With a look of complete bewilderment on his face, he swung the gate open and in drove Margaret and Billy Wallace in the little bubble car, both obviously amused by the look on the normally stolid policeman's face. The Princess, wrapped up tightly in her big fur coat made some comment to Billy as they drove in and they both burst into laughter, like two children who had played truant and didn't care who knew it. They drove up to the front door and sat there, still talking for a minute or more before Billy in his now rather crumpled dinner jacket, leaned over Margaret and opened the door at the front of the bubble car. I slipped back from the main gate and passed behind the car to get to the door to wait for the Princess.

With the door only slightly open, the Princess snuggled herself down in her seat and pulled the collar of her coat tight around her neck. Billy smiled at her, still holding the door, then she shrugged and leaned slowly forward and heaved herself lightly out of the machine. Standing now, she gave herself a discreet stretch, like a cat when it moves from one position to another, and waited for Billy to clamber out.

They walked toward me and came up to the step. And, in the brightness of day—for it was nearly 8 o'clock—they said their goodnights. They did not kiss or even shake hands but Margaret stifled a yawn and smiled: "Thank you, Billy. I did enjoy myself thoroughly. I'll call you later."

She watched the retreating figure of Mr. Wallace as he walked back to his car, then turned to me with unexpected brightness and said: "Good morning, John. Isn't it a lovely day?" And she walked jauntily into the house, slipping her mink from her shoulders to reveal a pale blue flowered satin cocktail dress. She looked pale and ever so slightly red-eyed. Her dress was creased, the make-up which she applied with such meticulous care was mostly gone and her hair had slipped a little from its normal grooming. That was my Princess in the cold light of the morning after the night before. And she looked utterly charming.

She went straight to the elevator and up to bed, not rising again until mid-afternoon.

Incidentally, another popular misconception about the social life of Royalty is that they get everything free. I have already explained that the Princess had to budget for her dresses. This was also true of her evenings out. Of course she herself did not pay, one of the escorts would foot the bill, but nothing was accepted which was not paid for except perhaps the traditional bottle of wine or champagne at table "with the manager's compliments." Otherwise, it cost her escort a pretty penny to take Margaret out for the evening. They always went to the very best and most expensive places and they were expected to settle the bill without any fuss and to leave a generous tip to the staff. Naturally, any restaurateur would have been delighted to waive the charge for anything connected with the Royal Family, but they were never allowed to do so, lest somebody abuse the fact.

The Princess herself never carried any money with her. She always took out an evening bag but it contained only her cigarettes, lighter, make-up and hankies. Margaret had her own bank account, however, and could, if she wished, write out her own checks. Occasionally, she and her Lady in Waiting, Iris Peake, would take a taxi down to London's West End shopping center and spend the afternoon browsing around the more expensive shops, returning with armsful of odds and ends for themselves.

Yet if Margaret bought anything, Miss Peake would always pay.

However, there was nothing Margaret liked more than to have a few coins in her pocket. Really, she had no need of money, much less small change, and there was no way in which she would be given small change. And it was because of this passion for something to rattle in her pocket that I became involved in some hilarious incidents with my Princess.

For one thing, I always had to provide her with the money to put in the collection plate whenever she went to church. If she was in Windsor Lodge or away on a weekend with friends, she would be expected to go to church on Sunday, and also expected to leave something fairly generous on the silver plate that morning. So she never failed to ask me to leave out her church money on Saturday night. I had to leave it in an envelope to be placed on her breakfast tray—a discreet plain envelope with the corner of a pound note sticking out.

And I, with my meager weekly wage, had to provide for my Princess. More than once, I have sighed over my last pound note as I took it from my pocket and slipped it into Margaret's breakfast envelope. I got it back, of course, when I claimed for it back at Clarence House. But that was not until the end of the month. At first, I assumed that she always put the pound into the collection tray, but one weekend when we were at Windsor, I found out to my huge amusement, that it was not as simple as that. Oh no. Margaret had to have her few shillings to jingle in her pocket.

As usual, I had left her pound in the envelope on her tray. But this particular Sunday morning, she rang for the Royal Lodge steward, a friend of mine, who had come down with the Queen Mother. As he told me later, he was surprised to have been called by Margaret as she normally asked for me. However, when he presented himself to her, she asked him: "Can you change this pound note for two ten shillings?"

The astonished steward dug into his wallet and was able

to produce the two smaller notes, handed them to her, and took her pound. My pound.

Then she said: "Thank you." And added, confidentially: "Don't tell John, will you?"

I'm afraid, however, that he was unable to resist telling me about the strange interlude, although I could not at that time understand why it had happened.

It was not until the following weekend that I got the answer to the little puzzle which had nagged at my mind all week. We were down at Royal Lodge again for the weekend and on Saturday night Margaret failed to ask for her church money and I quite forgot to put anything on her breakfast tray on Sunday morning. But nothing was mentioned and, as always, about 11:25, Margaret was ready to go to chapel, dressed in a dark gray costume with a pleated skirt and a rather fetching little white petaled hat. It was only when she had left the Lodge and was already walking down the gravel path, that I realized we had both apparently forgotten her donation money.

I panicked. I had a vision of the terrible embarrassment which the Princess might feel if she had to pass the collection plate in church that morning without making any donation, and, without stopping to think further, I ran out of the house after her. I saw the trim little figure striding down the path and I chased madly toward her.

Then I did something which I blush to remember. Without any formality at all, I yelled out: "Have you got your church money?" No "Your Royal Highness?" no "Ma'am." Margaret stopped abruptly and started to turn as I realized my horrible gaffe.

For a terrible moment I expected to get that cold, regal stare that Margaret could summon when she was angry with me. But no. To my amazement, she turned about and said very happily: "Yes, thank you, John." And off she trotted, leaving me even more puzzled.

By now, I was thoroughly intrigued to know where she had got her money, so I took the opportunity of mentioning it to Mrs. Gordon, who was down at the Lodge. I explained what I had done to the incredulous dresser. But when she explained something which had puzzled her, too, we both roared with laughter at this lovable antic of Margaret's.

It seemed that while Margaret was preparing for church,

Mrs. Gordon had seen her go, almost guilty, to her dressing table and rummage among the handkerchiefs, looking for something. She found it. It was a ten shilling note— the one, obviously, that she had changed with the steward the previous weekend. Seeing Mrs. Gordon there, the Princess looked at her, looked at the note in her hand, then almost defiantly, put it into the pocket of her jacket and walked out of the room.

Later on, when the Princess had returned from church, she called me into her room and I took the opportunity to raise the subject, with an explanation of why I had rushed after her down the path earlier in the day.

"I thought you must have forgotten your church money, Your Royal Highness," I explained.

"That's perfectly all right, John," she said. "Thank you for remembering."

"Then . . . you did have sufficient, Ma'am?" I persisted.

She shot me a quick glance. "Why, yes," she said. "I . . . er . . . I had it left over from last weekend." The last words tumbled off her tongue and she looked down to the floor.

"Yes, Ma'am," I replied, and smiled to myself.

But although Margaret liked to play little tricks like this to get a penny in her pocket, she was in fact a most generous person. It is worth repeating just one incident which throws some light on Margaret's spontaneous generosity. It was a little thing in itself, but quite revealing, I think.

It happened during the weekend of Armistice Sunday in November 1959. This is the Sunday nearest Nobember 11, when hostilities ceased at 11 a.m. in 1918, and it is used for a massive display of remembrance for all the dead in both World Wars. The Queen lays a wreath and all the other members of the Royal Family attend, although on this occasion, the wreath was laid by Prince Philip, because the Queen was at the time expecting her third child.

Traditionally too, everyone wears a poppy—the symbol of the grim years of war in France during 1914-1918. The day before the service at the Cenotaph in London's Whitehall, the poppysellers had called at Clarence House. These were rather special poppysellers—titled women known to the Royal Family, who gave up some of their time to help in this charity. Everyone in Clarence House sported one of these red and black emblems in their lapels and on their dresses.

Everyone, that is, except me. It was unfortunate, but when the poppysellers called I simply did not have a penny to my name. I was flat broke and to avoid embarrassment, I had to avoid the poppysellers. And of course, I looked conspicuously undecorated. I was conscious of this, quite naturally, and more so when I was next called to see the Princess in her room, for she herself had bought a big spray of three poppies and a sprig of fern and the whole posy was pinned to the breast of her black, flare-skirted dress.

She had given me my instructions about some errand or other and I was about to leave the room when she noticed my blue uniform was bare of a poppy.

"Where is it, John," she asked. "Where is your poppy?"

I felt my cheeks buring and knew that I blushed as I stammered: "Well, Your Royal Highness, I'm afraid . . . well, I just did not have any money when the ladies called at the House and I couldn't get one."

Margaret frowned in sympathy. Then a thought struck her.

"Then you shall have one of mine," she said firmly. She quickly unpinned her spray and began to unpick the wire binding. I murmured a protest, but she would have none of it. She carried on, but the poppy makers had done their job too well and it was too much for Margaret's long, manicured nails. She wrestled with it, frowned, and finally stamped her foot in annoyance. I was terribly touched at this out-of-the-blue offer from the Princess, but I could foresee that she would become quite cross if I allowed her to go on trying to undo the spray.

So, to preserve the moment, I interrupted: "That's all right, Ma'am. I am very grateful, but I can easily get a poppy from someone else. It is a pity to spoil your lovely spray."

My Princess smiled wryly; "I'm sorry, John," she said in half-apologetic tones. And she pinned the spray back on her dress.

I did manage to get hold of a poppy from someone or other as it happened, for I knew the Princess would notice had I not done so. But I shall always remember Margaret's charming gesture. I am reminded of it every November 11.

Of course, it would have been awful if the whole thing had been spoiled by one of Margaret's "paddies." Being a person of such rich pedigree, she was naturally a high-strung personality, but did not suffer overmuch from fits of temper. But she did have them, as anyone does, from time to time. And curiously enough, it was less than twenty-four hours after the poppy incident that she gave way to a burst of sheer crossness over something very trivial.

Nothing more, in fact, than a tube of glue. She had driven back from Whitehall, dressed suitably and somberly in black and had taken lunch at Clarence House. Even at that early stage, Christmas was in the air and during the afternoon, Margaret went to her sitting room to wrap some of the presents she had already bought for her friends and her hosts of relatives.

Halfway through that Sunday afternoon, she rang for me. On entering the room I was greeted by the lovely sight of Margaret at her desk, surrounded with boxes, paper parcels, string and brightly colored Christmas wrapping paper which had spilled on the floor around her feet.

She had been having a lovely time and her face was flushed with the excitement which, in a person of her nature, can be aroused by the giving as much as the receiving of presents. But when I inquired why she rang, she held up an empty tube which had contained a particular brand of glue.

"Can you get me some more of this stuff?" she asked.

I said I thought I could and went along to the pantry to look. I searched everywhere, in the cupboards, the drawers, in the kitchen, the steward's office, my own room and everywhere else I could think of. Half an hour later, I had been able to unearth only a pot of thin paper paste. It was the best I could manage, so I took it along to my Princess and offered it to her.

She looked at it scornfully. "No, no, no. That won't do at all," she said huffily. "Go to the chemist and get me a tube of the proper stuff. I must have it to do up these." And she waved her hand over the pile of parcels.

"But Your Royal Highness, today is Sunday and all the shops are shut."

She sighed with exasperation. "No, they are not all shut. There is a chemist's shop in Piccadilly which stays open twenty-four hours a day every day. Telephone them and tell them you must have a tube of this glue for me."

There was no room for further argument, so I accepted the order and withdrew, feeling not at all confident for I knew that this chemist's, although open, was only supposed to sell medical prescriptions.

In the pantry, I thumbed through the telephone book and found the number. A girl assistant answered.

"This is Clarence House," I said firmly. "I require a tube of glue." I felt a little foolish, but I gave her the name of the brand Margaret wanted. But the girl confirmed my previous thought, that the chemist's shop was open on Sunday only for medical requirements.

Then I played my trump card. "It's for Princess Margaret," I said. There was a pause and a second later, I could hear the rattle of the telephone receiver being put down. A moment later, a rather stern man's voice came on the line. He asked me what I wanted. With the certainty now that no one on earth would believe me, I repeated that I required a tube of So-and-So's glue for Princess Margaret.

Quite obviously the man thought I was a practical joker. "Are you pulling my leg?" he asked. And however much I tried to convince him, he quite patently did not believe me and capped the whole argument by telling me that the shop did not sell glue, and he rang off in my ear.

Heavily, I tramped back to the sitting room. Without glue, I thought, there would be fireworks. As gently as I could, I explained what had happened. I thought it might amuse her. But, oh dear, I was so wrong.

She jumped from her desk in a fury. "Oh, that stupid man," she cried. "What does he mean? Doesn't he think there is such a person as Princess Margaret?" And she marched up and down, grumbling to herself for two or three minutes while I stood there, trying my best to look sympathetic.

The Princess in a paddy was a lovely sight to behold, as a matter of fact. Her deep blue eyes sparkled and flashed and she tossed her head like a thoroughbred filly. And she usually simmered down after a few minutes. It was when she was coldly regal that she was really formidable. Then she had the ability to send shivers down my spine for I knew what to anticipate—a right Royal dressing down in an icy tone that made me feel that I wanted to creep into a hole in the ground.

This time, after her two minutes of "paddy" she cooled down quite abruptly.

"I'm sorry, John. Thank you for trying anyway," was all she said. And the storm was passed.

Chapter Nine

But to return to those earlier days and the Princess's escorts, those men chosen by Margaret from the members of her set to escort her on her nights out on London's West End.

Undoubtedly the favorite of these was Billy Wallace—the happy-go-lucky-millionaire man about town—who became the pick of the Margaret Set.

This man, more than all the others, was closest to my Princess at this time. And he topped this by being not only on close terms with the Princess, but also with the Queen Mother.

I often watched Billy Wallace in action and admired his knack of always keeping one step ahead of the rest of the conversation. If there were lags, it was Billy who came to the rescue and saved the Queen Mother from one of those dreadful silences which she so detested.

And believe me, the ability to do this was essential if one wanted to remain a member of the set for long. The Queen Mother, for all her charm, was not a great conversationalist with younger people. Many is the young man I have seen 'die' in her presence.

If the conversation flagged there could be a horrible silence and the Queen Mother would break it only by making her excuses—taking her dogs for a walk or something like that—and leaving the room. And woe betide the young man or woman who caused her to make such an embarrassing retreat. It meant being dropped from the set and of course, once this happened there was no returning.

But Billy could make her laugh and so often I have walked into the Clarence House drawing room and found the

Queen Mother and Margaret chuckling and giggling at one of Billy's jokes.

These informal meetings and discussions at Clarence House were nearly always lively affairs. With Billy's sparkling wit and with Dominic Elliott and Lord Plunkett to back him with general chit-chat, the Princess and Queen Mother could relax and join in the talk which ranged over a whole world of subjects.

My Princess never addressed any of her escorts as 'Mister'. Occasionally in an unguarded moment I heard her calling them 'Darling,' but this didn't happen often and had no real significance. Billy Wallace was Billy; Lord Plunkett was called Patrick and for Dominic Elliott she reserved the special nickname of 'Dom-Dom.'

For each of these regular escorts she would have a kiss when they called in the evening. But it was nothing more than a sisterly peck and always delivered to the side of the cheek.

And the men, in the house at least, were always careful to address Margaret with the rather formal 'Ma'am.'

Lord Plunkett I found, was a little apart from the other two and although he was often regarded as Margaret's official escort for the evening, they rarely went out together alone.

If Lord Plunkett arrived first at the house, I knew that there would be others joining him and Margaret before many minutes passed. And I was usually right.

I felt that she was never quite as fully at ease with Patrick as she was with the others, for some reason.

One evening I overheard a revealing conversation indicative of this between Her Royal Highness and the Honorable Iris Peake when they were planning an evening outing to the theatre, as they often did whenever Margaret found a gap in her normally full social diary.

Iris Peake had a piece of paper in her hand which I imagine contained the names of the people so far suggested, but they seemed to be having some difficulty in making up the number. Then Miss Peake suggested the name of Lord Plunkett.

I can't say that I ever really approved of Iris Peake and the way she chatted to My Princess but on this occasion I was interested to learn that she had other thoughts besides her friendship with Margaret.

Seven including Margaret had already agreed to go to the theatre outing. And she and Miss Peake were discussing whom to invite to make up the eighth.

Miss Peake was running through a list of suggested escorts —ticking them off on her fingers—when suddenly she stopped and looking up said to Margaret: "Why, what about Patrick? Surely he would like to come."

Her Royal Highness looked at her hard for a few seconds and then said with a slight smile: "Patrick—you mean Lord Plunkett."

"Yes Ma'm," replied Iris Peake. "Won't he do?"

Margaret pulled a face and giggled and said: "Of course you know he's not too fond of feminine company. He prefers to be with other men. I'm not sure that we ought to ask him."

But Iris Peake insisted. "Oh yes, Ma'm, I think we should. If ʏou like," and she colored a little, "he shall go as my partner."

Margaret managed to hide her surprise and said simply: "Very well. So it shall be." And I couldn't help noticing the pleased smile which came to Miss Peake's lips when she heard this.

It was obvious to me then why Margaret was not happy with Patrick as an escort. . . .

Throughout the first six months I spent as personal footman to Her Royal Highness I heard and read many rumors linking the Princess's name with those of Billy Wallace, Dominic Elliott and, much to my amusement, Lord Plunkett. But from my privileged position inside Clarence House I was able to dismiss these rumors as mere idle gossip and was able to watch with amusement Margaret's reaction to the speculative gossip in the diary columns of the morning newspapers.

At this time I, more than anyone else, knew the real relationship between Margaret and her three most popular escorts. It was only friendship between Margaret and these talented and amusing young men, based on a mutual interest in good conversation, good food and the arts.

Before the appearance of Mr. Antony Armstrong-Jones— who in my opinion will never match the wit and intelligence of Margaret's earlier escorts—Her Royal Highness spent many weekends in the company of these at house parties in Royal Lodge Windsor.

She was rarely seen at Clarence House during the weekends. If she didn't go to Windsor Royal Lodge she would visit friends in the country or make trips to Balmoral and Sandringham as a guest of the Queen.

I looked forward to these trips away from London and the semi-pompous atmosphere in Clarence House which persisted even below stairs in the servants' hall.

After my first unhappy experience with the other servants —they never really accepted me as one of them—I kept myself strictly apart. They did not trust me with their secrets, possibly because I would not agree to turn a blind eye to the inevitable backstairs fiddling which went on in any big household.

So I was always unhappy if my Princess decided to go out of town for the weekend and I was not included in her party. It would mean two days' solitary confinement for me in my tiny bedroom, as I was not welcomed or invited to join in the amusement organized by my fellow servants at Clarence House.

But a trip out of London with my mistress never failed to bring me happiness and a sense of release which usually continued well into the following week after our return to the House.

Margaret had many favorite weekend hideaways but it was in the peaceful friendly atmosphere of Windsor Royal Lodge that she really relaxed.

During these weekends Margaret indulged her love of sport—horseback riding, swimming in an open air pool, dancing in the lounge or more often than not just wandering in jumper and slacks through the wooded park land in Windsor Great Park.

I remember it was on one of these weekends away—it was actually at the Devonshire house of Margaret's cousin, Mrs. Ann Rhodes and her husband—that I realized how strong was my Princess's insistence on Malvern water with her drink.

This ridiculous habit of always taking Malvern water had often caused me trouble and embarrassment, not to mention an occasional tongue-lashing, throughout my service with her. Now I was to see someone else put on the spot by my Princess' petty refusal to drink plain tap water.

It was on the evening of our arrival. I had immediately started unpacking. The Princess had changed and with her host and hostess and a few other guests was about to take a pre-dinner drink.

The drink tray had been placed on a side table and Mr. Denys Rhodes was playing host. Of course, none of the other guests could be served until Margaret had made her choice.

I had gone into the room with a case of records from the Princess's luggage which she wanted the others to hear and witnessed what took place next. It was warm in the room and I could see that the Princess was looking a little weary after our long journey down from London. I knew that at this moment she would be looking forward to her usual whisky and water before eating.

And I was not mistaken. Mr. Rhodes turned to Margaret as I stepped across the room with the phonograph records in my arms and through a lull in the conversation I heard him say: "What will you have to drink Ma'm?" Came the answer: "Whisky and water, please."

"Certainly," said Mr. Rhodes and reached across to the drink tray and picked out a fresh bottle of whisky. After giving Margaret's glass a generous helping he raised a crystal jug filled with ordinary water and was obviously about to add it to my Princess's drink.

Instinctively I pushed forward to warn him. But I was too late. Before I could speak the Princess had spotted what he was doing and in a voice which stilled all other conversation in the room said:

"No Denys. Not that. I want water in my whisky."

There was complete silence in the room. No one knew what the Princess was talking about. That was obvious to me. But they seemed to be hoping—by the look on their faces—that they were about to witness a Royal tantrum.

Mr. Rhodes was apparently quite puzzled too. He looked at Margaret as if she might have been joking and with a slight smile playing about his lips said: "But this is water, Ma'm."

But Margaret wasn't having any of that, as I could have told him. She looked him up and down and completely ignoring the rest of the company said in her most Royal tones: "That is not water. It is only tap water."

Then she caught sight of me and beckoned me over. I pushed my way through the group of people to her side. They just stood and stared at the three of us—my Princess, Major Rhodes, and myself.

"John," said Princess Margaret, "knows exactly what I mean." Then, turning to me she directed: "Fetch my special water here immediately, will you?" When I left to go to the kitchen Mr. Rhodes was looking perplexed. He must have thought Margaret or himself was not quite all there.

In the kitchen I went to the corner where I had placed Margaret's Malvern water and picked a bottle from the crate. As an after thought I lifted a bottle of Margaret's favorite brand of whisky from a cardboard carton which we always carried with us on trips out of town and went back to where Margaret was waiting.

When I reached the room the other guests were still silent. And I realized why immediately when I heard Mrs. Rhodes say in a slightly vexed voice: "But Margaret, water is water wherever it comes from. You've got to admit that."

Mrs. Rhodes had come to the aid of her bewildered husband who was leaning against the table that held the drink tray. I didn't hear the Princess's reply, but took the bottle of Malvern water over to her and showed it to her. It was still sealed; Margaret always insisted on this. On seeing it she smiled and nodded her head, and turning to her cousin, Mrs. Rhodes, said: "This, Ann, is water. Now do you see what I mean?"

I undid the seal in front of her—another rule she invariably insisted on—and took it over to the drink tray. I poured away the whisky Mr. Rhodes had poured for my Princess and opening the fresh bottle I had brought from the kitchen prepared a fresh drink.

With all eyes on me I added some Malvern water and with a slight bow presented it to Princess Margaret. She smiled and sipped it. Then, still smiling, she nodded her head slightly towards me which was a sign that everything was all right.

Then she gave a little gesture with her hand, grinned at Mr. Rhodes, who still seemed to be puzzling out the difference in the two waters, and the party went on. . . .

This type of demonstration of stubbornness by my Princess never failed to amuse me, especially if it concerned her love of Malvern water. But I soon learned that Margaret could not recognize the taste of Malvern water from any other kind. It was only a Royal whim that made her an addict to this particular liquid.

Though at the time of the Rhodes episode I had been very dignified and had fully backed my Princess in her wish, there were times in the kitchen or in my own room at Clarence House that I just sat and roared with laughter at incidents with the ridiculous water.

I have to confess now that several times on similar weekends in the country or away from Clarence House and London we actually ran out of fresh Malvern water. This was a piece of carelessness on my part which would have earned me a right Royal dressing down if my Princess had ever learned about it.

And I knew that if a fresh bottle had not been produced when called for there would be a stern reproach for me from the Princess. She had decided that without the Malvern water she could not drink whisky and therefore I was depriving her of a decent drink. That is how Margaret's mind worked.

So it was left for me to do the best I could when drinks were imminent. And doing the best I could often meant being dishonest with Princess Margaret. It happened several times that I was forced to take an empty bottle from the crate and then hunt around the kitchen for a used Malvern seal. This could mean sorting through the rubbish in the waste bin or grubbing about on the kitchen floor.

Then after making sure that none of the other servants were about, I would fill the empty bottle with cold tap water and carefully fit the seal in place. A little glue and some gentle re-arranging of the red and white paper seal and it would look as good as new.

Of course my Princess never spotted it. She would check the seal when I showed it to her but, trusting me as she did, she never bothered to scrutinize the seal closely.

I always felt a little guilty at fooling her but she drank her whisky and "water" as usual and never showed any ill effects. In fact sometimes I would swear she appeared to enjoy it more than the real thing.

There was one weekend particularly which will always stick out in my mind when I had to improvise to make do. But it had nothing to do with water or the Princess's fancies.

It was on the weekend that Her Royal Highness paid a visit to Mrs. Rhodes' elderly mother—the seventy-five year old sister of the Queen Mother, Lady Elphinstone. This was, I think, the eldest of Margaret's aunts and I know she was the strangest I ever came up against.

Lady Elphinstone lived in a gaunt, ramshackle old mansion which sprawled across its own grounds just outside the town of Musselburgh in Scotland. She was an old lady and lived completely alone in the huge building except for a cook and a daily cleaning woman.

When we arrived with the Princess's party we were astonished to find that there were no electric light bulbs in the house and what was more important, no heating.

A chauffeur was sent to the town with instructions to buy two dozen bulbs. There were provisions for this form of lighting but for some reason Lady Elphinstone just let the bare sockets hang from the ceiling and used candles for lighting.

When the chauffeur returned he was put to work on the electric generator—the house was not on the general electricity supply—and told he must get it started before dinner. Meanwhile, as the Princess sat chatting politely with her hostess, Mrs. Gordon had been shown Margaret's room.

Poor Mrs. Gordon; she was horrified. I shall never forget the stricken look on her face when she came running down to tell me about the "dungeon" which had been put aside for our Royal Mistress.

"Oh my goodness," she gasped. "It is dark, damp, dreary and cold. Her Royal Highness cannot possibly sleep in a room like that. You must do something about it and quickly. I will leave it to you."

It was dreary all right, and would have to stay that way. I reckoned it would take at least a week's work to get the place looking reasonable for my Princess. But the cold and damp and light . . . those I could do something about. My answer was an old dust-covered kerosene heater.

And, much to Mrs. Gordon's disgust, when we installed it in Margaret's bedroom great clouds of smoke and soot belched out. But it was better than nothing and would help to take the chill and dampness out of the air.

It was typical of this topsy turvy house—a relic from the dark ages I imagined—that dinner was served not in the dining room on the first floor where everything was covered in dust sheets, but in the downstairs library.

It was my lot to do all the arranging for the meal as I was the only person in the house capable of serving dinner to a Princess. In fact I found myself in charge of everything.

I fitted a naked bulb into the single light socket in the center of the ceiling and examined the table closely. I was shocked. The table could not possibly be used to serve a meal because it was sticky with damp. I wondered how on earth Lady Elphinstone in her advanced years could have lived in that house without catching pneumonia or some other fatal disease.

I found a thick white tablecloth in the kitchen, and spread that over the damp wood. And then came my biggest shock of all. I could not find the best cutlery. All I could see in the ancient kitchen cabinet was an old bone-handled set.

Thinking Lady Elphinstone kept the best silver locked away, I went to look for her. I approached the lady and, putting my lips within a foot of her ear, bellowed: "Where is the cutlery my lady?"

Lady Elphinstone cocked an eyebrow in the direction of the kitchen and said haughtily: "It is all in the kitchen, my man. Where do you expect it to be?" So bone handles it had to be.

I carefully scrubbed the old cutlery and set the table for four people: the Princess, Lady Elphinstone, the Lady in Waiting Lady Elizabeth Cavendish, and the Princess's private secretary Major Francis Leigh.

But worse was to come. Search though I did I could find only one knife, one fork and one soup spoon each. Consequently when the party had eaten their grapefruit—with a soup spoon—I had to run into the kitchen between serving the other course to wash them in time to have them back on the table by the dessert. But no one seemed to notice or if they did nothing was said.

The meal was eaten in gloom and had I been less busy trying to maintain a semblance of good taste I would probably have found the whole series of incidents very amusing.

On the table there was only one set of cruets instead of the one apiece which the Princess was used to seeing at

Clarence House and this was shuttled across the table in a most un-Royal way.

They shared a single half bottle of table wine between the four of them. That was just half a glass each. Throughout the meal the Princess sat hunched in her chair with a thick woollen cardigan wrapped tightly about her. And I noticed the slightly pained expression which came to her face whenever she glanced at the huge empty and unlit fireplace.

My Princess must have been feeling very cold but with the usual show of Royal dignity she wasn't going to show it. Especially since Lady Elphinstone didn't seem to know the cold existed.

My Princess could also see from her seat the large window with its thick iron bars fixed to the frame and she shuddered and turned away and went on with her meal. I have rarely seen her looking so unhappy.

It proved to be the shortest meal I had ever served Princess Margaret. The whole thing was over in twenty minutes flat and the party retired quickly to the drawing room and the little comfort which it offered.

I had somehow found time between my other jobs, before the guests went upstairs to change for dinner, to light a small fire in the drawing room, much to the cook's disgust since her reaction to the cold was the same as her mistress's.

Now, as the guests filed inside, they smiled a little at the pleasant and unexpected luxury of a coal fire. But their pleasure was short-lived. The fire was not a success—partly due to a warning I had received from the cook when I lit it before the meal.

She had told me not to build it too high in case the chimney, unswept for years and rarely used, caught fire and the whole house burned down. Even with the fire, the damp which had seeped into every item of furniture in the house over a series of decades was not dispersed.

Now the fire spluttered and crackled despondently in the hearth and I noticed tiny wisps of steam curling up from the carpet in front of the hearth.

But Margaret could not be cowed by the circumstances surrounding her. She must have seen the funny side of that day's events, because after dinner she shrugged off her miserable mood and ignoring the dismal surroundings enlivened the evening with jokes and funny stories which kept them all amused until they went to bed at 11 o'clock.

By far the biggest shock to me came during the evening. I have mentioned what Margaret's room was like, but what a shock I got when I went up to look at my own. It was not really on the second floor but up a few stairs off the ground floor.

I walked slowly along a stone-flagged hall and shivered at the noise of my footsteps echoing around its tall white walls and ceiling. The air was damp and the cold struck through my thin-soled shoes.

When I reached the door to my room I paused, and looked about me. I did not feel at ease in that house. Then I turned to inspect the large old wooden door which guarded the entrance to my bedroom. It creaked at my touch and I pushed it open wide.

I took in the bare wooden boarded floor and stark white walls and ceiling. I wondered, is my Princess to sleep in a similar room tonight? The thought made me shiver even more.

The room had nothing to offer in the way of warmth. This was a far cry from the room I occupied in Clarence House. Though bare, that was still livable.

I would not have invited my worst enemy to sleep in this room. But to make a fuss would have earned me a rebuke from my Princess and I decided even though I would have to spend a cold and sleepless night in the house at Musselburgh I would not complain. I knew that Princess Margaret too would be sleeping under conditions to which she was not accustomed. If she could bear it, I thought, so could I.

So having decided to make the best of an exceedingly bad job, I inspected my quarters. The bed was the first object to which I turned my notice. It had a big brass bedstead which creaked as I rested my head against one post. Stories I had heard of collapsing beds in strange old houses flooded back to me and again an icy tingle crept up and down my back.

But I shrugged them off, reminding myself that Margaret would not be frightened to spend her night alone and neither must I be. Even so, as I gingerly lowered myself on the bulky, uncomfortable straw-filled mattress, I made ready to leap off again should the bed start to give way.

It didn't. I prodded the mattress and heard the ancient and rickety springs groaning underneath. Such is Royal service, I thought. It is worse than anything I encountered in the Marines. I looked around again. Not for me the niceties of a modern bathroom, I thought, as I spotted the large bowl and jug, both earthenware, on a bulky chest of drawers.

I expected to find the jug empty. But it wasn't. I dipped three fingers of my right hand in the lip and almost gasped with the shock. The jug was filled with icy cold water. I withdrew my numbed fingers and sucked them as I wandered around the rest of the room.

There was nothing else of interest to hold my attention so I returned to the kitchen and sat down to supper with a blue-nosed Mrs. Gordon. She too was feeling the cold and had very little to say in praise of our elderly hostess.

It was over this meal in the kitchen that I heard my Princess's comments on our hostess's hospitality. We had to use the same cutlery as the Royal party to eat our meal. It had been hurriedly washed after them, a fact which caused Mrs. Gordon to give a sniff of disapproval.

Then suddenly she turned to me and said: "The Princess has told me that she would not like to stay here for any length of time. But as it is only for one night, she is prepared to grin and bear it. After all, it is better than having to sleep on a train in some siding or other."

If the Princess thought that, I said to myself, then I would have to disagree with her. A bed in a nice warm railway car would be preferable to the miserable drafty room which had been set aside for me.

I remembered this again later when I found myself in bed huddled in my two blankets trying to keep out the cold. But drafts managed to find their way in under the covers, however I arranged them, and I spent a restless night.

The following morning the whole party rose early, mainly because like myself they had dozed only fitfully during the night and had been glad to leave their cold beds and dress in warm clothes.

When I woke dawn was streaking in through the window and I was stiff. But I leaped quickly out of bed and rinsed my hands and face in the cold water in the jug. It was only a rub but I promised myself a good wash later when some warm water would be available. By the time my Princess came down I had helped cook prepare a light meal and using the bone-handled cutlery again the party sat down for its last meal in the house.

Before Margaret and her guests departed I saw Lady Elphinstone pull my Princess over to one side and heard her say: "I shall be coming down to Clarence House to see you shortly. But please when you go back give my regards to your dear mother, Her Majesty Queen Elizabeth." Then they kissed and parted. Margaret looking happy again now that she was leaving the house. She led her guests out to the waiting cars and we drove away.

I remember looking back at the bleak house and seeing the tiny figure of Lady Elphinstone standing in the great doorway. Then she turned on her heel and disappeared. It was one place where I did not want to make a return journey with my Royal mistress.

This was one side of my gay young Princess which the general public did not know—those informal weekends with her friends away from the formality and strict protocol of much of her life at Clarence House.

Her "let's get away from it all" attitude seemed to affect all her close circle of friends and servants including myself. Whenever things seemed to be getting the best of her Princess Margaret always managed to escape for a few days from the seemingly endless list of Royal engagements.

But there was nothing Princess Margaret loved better than a party. Any excuse was good enough. Often she didn't even bother to invent one. Occasionally she would invite a few of her friends in to her sitting room at Clarence House when she found herself in the party mood and keep them there—protests or not—until well past midnight.

When she gave parties champagne would flow freely. And it would only be the best. Margaret was never mean when it came to giving people a good time.

Her Royal Highness would warn me in the afternoon if such a party was planned and would say how many friends would be coming. Then I would go down and put a few bottles of champagne on ice.

The first such shindig I attended produced something of a surprise for me. In the diary or gossip columns of the English newspapers I had often read accounts of Margaret's outings in London's West End and how she had been see drinking champagne. Now I learned that those stories could not have been completely true.

Throughout my service with her as her personal footman I never saw my Princess touch a drop of the liquid. During the evenings when champagne was being drunk I would offer a glass to her. But always she pushed me away with a polite refusal. "No thank you John," she would say. "You know I never drink this," and she would ask me for another whisky and water. That was the only drink which I saw her take and enjoy during the evening.

But the Princess was really in her element when she could dress up in one of her fabulous new gowns and spend the evening dancing until the early hours of the following morning.

It was soon after our return from the annual trip to Balmoral in 1959—that is the Scottish retreat where the whole Royal Family goes every year for the grouse season—that I heard the Queen Mother had decided to hold an informal dance within the walls of Clarence House itself.

This promised to be a splendid affair and my dreams turned out to be correct. It was to be one of the most glittering nights of my life. In all, more than two hundred and fifty people were invited. Even an informal dance held by Royalty was an important occasion. The men would be in their dinner jackets and the women in their evening dresses and bedecked with sparkling diamonds and other precious jewels.

It was one of the occasions when I was to come up against the Queen. She had been asked personally by her mother to attend and she was obviously pleased to be there. But Prince Philip did not attend. I learned later that he was away on private business at the time and could not get back.

Her Majesty the Queen Mother, Her Royal Highness Princess Alexandra, my own beautiful Princess, and the Queen completed a fabulous Royal quartet.

All that day preparations for the dance were going on in the House. It was to be held in the huge chandelier-lit and fairy-like first floor drawing room. For days crates of many different kinds of drink and massive hampers of food had been arriving in the kitchens.

I helped some of the other Royal servants to roll back the Persian carpets to make a good floor for dancing and push the heavy settees against the walls to give room in the middle. Over a dozen tables were set up in the corridor outside the door for the drinks. There was a great deal of chatter among the servants and much speculation about the person Margaret would choose from among her escorts to be her partner.

Even though we were accustomed to the lavishness of the Royal entertainment we were astounded to see how much drink was being brought in for the guests. In all, one hundred and twenty bottles of champagne were kept on ice for the champagne bar. A barman behind the counter chuckled at the simplicity of the job he had been asked to do that evening since that was the only drink he would be expected to serve.

At the liquor bar in another part of the drawing room hundreds of bottles of spirits, liqueurs and wines had been stacked in preparation for the inevitable rush which would be made on this counter before the evening was out.

Because of the number of people who had been invited, it was necessary to bring in extra staff. Many of these were recruited from Buckingham Palace to help out by serving drinks in the drawing room and to run the buffet which had been set up in the dining room on the ground floor.

We servants wore our semi-state liveries which were scarlet-tailed coats with gleaming gilt buttons and gold epaulettes hanging from the left shoulder. In direct contrast to this splendid—yet to those who wore it ridiculous—uniform were our white ties and long black trousers.

Resplendent though these liveries seemed to the guests, to those who had to wear them they were uncomfortable and impractical. And I, though proud to wear the uniform of my Princess and carry her crest, always felt an object of amusement to those who saw me.

But I was lucky. At Buckingham Palace the servants were often called upon to dress up like so many dolls. On an occasion such as this at the Palace the servants would have had to wear full state livery. This meant scarlet coats, tight blue velvet knee-breeches, white stockings and black patent leather shoes with highly polished silver buckles.

I always thanked my lucky stars that I was never called upon to wear this outfit which linked us with the royal servants of earlier centuries. But that does not mean that I was not issued with such a uniform. I was.

I had received one of these dolls outfits when first I became a member of the Clarence House staff. This was in addition to the ordinary everyday uniform. I laughed and laughed when I saw myself in the mirror in my room with the scarlet coat trailing from my waist. But I never bothered to even try on the rest of this outfit and after that first day locked it away in a cupboard, in the hope that I would never have to wear it.

Luckily, I never did. For an even more uncomfortable extra was needed for state livery. Whenever it was worn, I discovered servants were obliged to plaster their hair with a revolting white paste used in place of the more traditional powdered wig.

This was really an economy on the part of the Royal Household—an economy which brought a great deal of trouble and inconvenience to the unfortunate servants at the Palace. Powdered wigs, I discovered, were terribly expensive and a favorite nesting place of moths. They decided it would be cheaper to pay the staff threepence a day extra. And for this the unfortunate men had to walk about all day with a gluey mixture in their hair.

For this threepence a day they had to rise at 7 o'clock, spread the foul stuff on their heads, and brush it in. This would be left in their hair all day until they washed it out before going to bed, often fifteen or sixteen hours later.

Sometimes when important personages from abroad came to the Palace the unfortunate servants would have to go through this revolting and uncomfortable procedure some three or four days in succession—all for a mere nine-pence or a shilling extra in their pay envelope.

It was because of this that one or two of the servants at Buckingham Palace quit their jobs. And there is nothing that any of the remainder can do to have these conditions changed.

But the semi-state uniform, though not as gaudy, did look very impressive. I spent some hours during the day of the dance preparing my livery—pressing it so that I would look my very best and a credit to Princess Margaret and her household. I went up to change and spent from 5:30 on preening myself before the mirror before going down to receive the guests.

But this was not to be. Instead of my usual position at

the front door I had been switched over to run one of the champagne bars which had hurriedly been set up in the first floor corridor outside the drawing room.

By this time my Princess had gone to bed for an hour, and I envied her because I knew that the dance would go on into the early hours of the following morning and we would all begin to feel a little tired.

But with that short nap in the evening Margaret was preparing herself, and I knew that she would be among the last to show any trace of tiredness.

I did not see Her Royal Highness again until about 7 o'clock that evening. I had taken up my position for the evening behind the makeshift bar counter in the corridor. Soon after I arrived and checked the drinks and glasses Margaret and Queen Elizabeth, the Queen Mother, came down together.

My Princess was positively bouncing with excitement. This was her kind of evening. A dance was something to be enjoyed and I could see from her suppressed excitement that she was well prepared to get as much as she could out of the night's entertainment. At this stage there was still no escort by her side and I again wondered who the lucky man would be who would be her partner.

She looked very beautiful that night. Her petite frame was swathed in a full length oyster pink satin gown with an off-the-shoulder neckline. I almost gasped out loud when I saw the necklace she was wearing. It must have been priceless. A simple string of flawless diamonds. She wore diamond pendant earrings, a matching diamond bracelet and a tiny gold wrist watch.

Her hairdresser had called at the House earlier that evening to give her dark locks a final setting and it provided a wonderful framework for her delicately featured face.

The make-up of course was exactly right. Not overdone, not lacking. As always, Margaret had done this part of her toilet herself and that evening she proved her skill. Without bias I thought my Princess was the most beautiful woman present at the dance.

As the couple, mother and daughter, stepped slowly and daintily down the corridor I thought to myself, was there ever such a couple? In contrast with Margaret's simple beauty the Queen Mother was at her most splendid.

A slight smile played about her lips and her eyes sparkled

with anticipation. She looked utterly regal in a pale pink dress overlayed with yard upon yard of fluffy tulle. She, like Margaret, had chosen to wear diamonds to set off her ensemble. A glittering chain of these gems interspersed with pearl drops tumbled about her neck and diamonds and pearls flashed at her ears.

The couple chatted gaily as they walked past me and then went on from spot to spot checking to see that everything was in order and that all the servants were properly garmented. I thought to myself as they swept past the champagne bar that my Princess looked like a girl who had just arrived at her first ball.

The next hour sped by. Gradually the guests trickled into the drawing room and by 8 o'clock the first strains of music wafted out onto the corridor. Through the open doors I saw a few couples who, glasses in hand were promenading around the floor.

Soon the Lancaster Room on the ground floor next to Princess Margaret's sitting room, which was being used as a cloak room, was a collector's dream of fabulous mink coats and wraps which must have been worth a small fortune.

Slowly the house filled with the noise of clinking glasses, music and laughter. The whole building seemed to have come alive. The gleaming lights in the grand corridor and the soft reflections cascaded down from the giant chandeliers in the drawing room on the waiting couples.

At 9:30 Princess Margaret preceded by the Queen Mother, came up the grand staircase, after their supper at the buffet downstairs, and then came the moment that everyone had been waiting for. The music struck up once again and Margaret and her mother led off the dancing. Soon the floor became crowded as late-comers arrived and joined the dance.

I was working flat out behind the champagne bar. As fast as one person was served someone else was there to take his place. The noise of the champagne corks popping made my bar sound like a shooting gallery.

It must have been almost 10 o'clock when the Queen arrived with Lord Plunkett, deputy comptroller of Buckingham Palace household, as escort. It seemed strange to see Lord Plunkett offering his arm to the Queen instead of her sister, my Princess.

I did not notice her arrival at the main door but caught

my first glimpse of her between the crush at the bar as she mounted the grand staircase and, with Lord Plunkett in attendance, walked across the corridor toward my champagne counter.

The crowd hurriedly stood aside as the Queen approached and fell silent. As she passed between their ranks the gentlemen bowed and the ladies did a slight curtsey towards her.

She stopped directly in front of me and then cast an amused frown at the debris of empty bottles, scattered corks and half-full glasses before her.

The Queen looked straight at me and said in a low voice: "May I have a glass of champagne please?"

I did not know it then or I might have been more flustered in serving her but the next time the Queen was to speak to me her voice would be raised in anger and I would bear the brunt of a flaming royal rage.

But at the time I was so overcome at being spoken to by my Queen that I could only gasp out: "Yes. Of course, Your Majesty." And I reached for a fresh bottle of champagne.

The Queen laughed as the cork popped out and reached to take the glass full of the bubbling liquid I had poured. She sipped it and then indicated that I should pour out a glass for her escort.

I had thought Margaret and the Queen Mother were splendidly dressed but the Queen's ensemble shamed even theirs. She was wearing a gorgeous dress of cream satin with dozens of pearls sewed on it. She too had chosen to wear diamond jewelry and dangled an evening bag of the same material as her dress from one wrist.

There was not the slightest sign to show that the Queen was pregnant, although within a few short months the whole world was to know that a new baby Prince had been born to her—Prince Andrew.

They stood at the bar counter, the Queen and Lord Plunkett, talking softly and sipping their drinks. By this time the crowd had got over their excitement at seeing the Queen and a general hum of conversation swelled again in the corridor. The Queen seemed very relaxed and happy. I had rarely seen her before in such good humor. I noticed that after a few minutes she became a trifle restless and kept glancing across to the doors of the drawing room. Then I realized what she was looking for. The Queen Mother and

Princess Margaret must have known of the Queen's arrival but neither of them had turned up to greet her.

But then I saw them hurrying through the crush to her side. The Queen was all smiles when they spoke, and including Lord Plunkett in their circle the foursome stood and chatted for nearly fifteen minutes in front of me. The Queen Mother and her two daughters made a charming picture as they stood there talking animatedly above the noise. At one point I saw Margaret, always full of fun, lead the others in a burst of boisterous laughter, holding on to her sister's arm as she did so.

Soon they were all laughing. Margaret had a wonderful gift of being able to make other people happy even though she may have been in a miserable mood herself—as did happen on occasion.

Then I heard the Queen say to Margaret and her mother: "I would like to go in to the dancing now. Shall we?"

"Yes, of course," laughed Margaret and she led the way in to the drawing room, turning every few seconds to laugh with her sister at a private joke. All three danced for hours and every time I had occasion to go into the drawing room I looked out for Margaret. Each time she was with a different partner and always smiling and chattering away.

During the evening she came out to my bar with the Queen two or three times and each time they were both flushed with excitement and high spirits. But the highlight of the evening came later. It was a truly fantastic sight to us all. Especially to the servants, who had seen the Royal family in a relaxed mood, but still expected them to be pretty regal in company outside the family.

It started when the Queen Mother went over to bandleader, Ray Ellington, and asked him to play a conga. Then she hurried across to her two daughters and Alexandra and the rest and urged them all to follow her as she led a swaying, laughing, noisy conga line round the room.

Out of the room they came, laughing and shrieking with excitement. Then the Queen Mother wth the Queen and Princess Margaret behind her jogged along the corridor in time to the music and then tripped lightly down the main stairs. The music got louder and louder and Ray Ellington tried to make it audible to the Royal party some hundreds of yards away.

Round about and back up again to the first floor they jostled in the greatest display of letting-the hair-down that I have ever seen. Holding on to one another's hips they coasted back to the drawing room and broke up in howls of laughter.

I couldn't resist peeping round the door to see how the Queen had taken it. She was holding her mother's arm and smiling. Margaret was almost doubled up in a fit of uncontrolled mirth. The Queen Mother, looking slightly red in the face, was panting a little, but her face was lit with a great beam of happiness and she stretched out an arm and drew her two daughters close to her.

This glorious sight of the conga line led by Margaret's mother and sister literally stopped the ball for a few minutes, and while the band rested the Queen and her mother came to my bar again with Princess Alexandra. Margaret was still talking to Lord Plunkett in the drawing room.

Princess Alexandra wore a startling tulip style dress of orange with a green fern motif. She and my Princess danced almost non-stop throughout the long night with an ever changing variety of partners.

The dance went on until almost 3 o'clock the next morning. Then tables were arranged in the ground floor main corridor with portable stoves on them. From then on it was bacon and egg breakfasts served to order. This was taken with either champagne or black coffee depending on the stamina of the guests. By 4 o'clock the Queen Mother and Margaret had taken up their positions at the main door to the House and were seeing the guests out personally.

Dozens of cars were waiting in convoy outside with sleepy drivers at the wheels. They had had to wait in the cars most of the night for their masters and mistresses. The front door was a confusion of people talking at the tops of their voices and footmen trying hard to persuade them gently to go to their cars.

When the last of the guests had departed and the Princess and her mother had said all their goodbys, the great door to the House were closed and bolted and the gates were closed by the policemen on duty at the lodge. One or two early morning workers paused in the Mall to watch the line of cars move off and then resumed their paths to their offices and shops.

The Queen Mother and Princess Margaret still had spirit enough after seeing off their guests to make a full round of the House to say their thank you's to the servants before they retired to their beds.

Once the Royal couple were out of sight we all loosened the stiff collars of our suits and tucked in to our own breakfasts. Everything was washed down with champagne. We lingered half an hour over this meal, then settled down to hardest work of the night. We had to get the house in order again for the coming day. What a mess everywhere. I found champagne glasses down behind chairs, resting on the stairs and hidden behind ornaments.

At daybreak the house snapped back into routine and the Queen Mother was called as usual at 7:30 a.m. But the Princess, worn out by her exertions of the previous evening was exhausted and slept on, as was her custom after such an occasion, until mid-day.

The extra servants left the house after the last of the mess had been cleared away and went home to their beds. But the Clarence House staff were not so lucky. Red-eyed and worn out though most of us were we still had to stay on duty all that day until late at night.

At the back of the house, the trash cans bulged with broken plates, glasses and scraps of food and literally hundreds of empty bottles—the usual sort of debris of any party increased about one hundredfold.

That was all that was left of one of the most fabulous evenings of my life. I saw Margaret later in the day and she was rather subdued. She pottered around the house during the afternoon, wrote a few letters and sat dozing by a fire in her sitting room. She did not go out. And she did not contact the Queen Mother, who for her part I learned was bustling round her quarters full of her usual bubbling energy.

Fortunately for me, since I was beginning to feel very tired myself. Margaret did not stay up late that night and I was not required after 10:30.

So I retired to my room, threw my uniform in a heap at the bottom of the bed and crawled in between the sheets. I lay awake for a time and gradually, as sleep came, the mixed figures of the Queen, the Queen Mother and my Princess became more hazy as I saw them doing a conga over the roofs of Buckingham Palace and off into the night.

Then, the light still blazing, my eyes slowly closed and I dropped off into a deep sleep.

Chapter Ten

The evening of the grand ball came toward the end of what I call Margaret's escort era. With the Townsend episode out of her system she threw herself in to a hectic round of high life in the nightclubs and the parties of the upper set.

The West End of London knew Margaret as a regular visitor and every top club-goer in town began to recognize hers as a friendly face—one of the regulars.

But this sort of life couldn't go on forever and I think there was some pressure put on Margaret from the Palace to try and persuade her to give up this hectic and much publicized night life.

And gradually as memories of Peter Townsend and his shock engagement faded I saw Margaret undergo a gradual change. Her trips into the West End clubs became less frequent. She concentrated more on the theatre and quieter pursuits and her choice of escorts became more limited.

A new face was creeping into the picture—the face of a dapper young man with a wave in his hair and a camera never very far from his hand. Tony Armstrong-Jones had made his entry and Margaret was neglecting her other escorts. And during the weeks which followed I saw the first seeds of love planted which would finally bring this young man and my Princess to the altar in Westminster Abbey.

By the time the Royal Family had returned from their summer trip to Balmoral, Antony Armstrong-Jones was making regular appearances at Clarence House. He had been with the Princess at Balmoral and that alone had confirmed the suspicions I had about some deeper feeling between Margaret and Tony.

Margaret had known Tony for about two years by this time and I knew that he had taken her out occasionally in recent months, but had always thought of him as being merely a fringe member of the very exclusive Margaret set. And no one, not even I, would seriously have thought at that time of linking the name of Princess Margaret with that of this society photographer and ex-newspaperman.

As a friend, yes. But he was still a commoner and no match, so we all thought, for the Princess. But how wrong we all were was proved to the world within a few months and to myself within a few weeks.

It was during the latter half of that year of so many memories that I began to see more and more of young Tony and less and less of the old group of Royal "favorites". The Wallaces, the Elliotts and the Plunketts were on the way out and it was Tony more and more to whom Margaret turned when she needed an escort. And gradually I came to feel that I was unknowingly sharing a secret which they were keeping from the rest of the world.

In the ensuing months I was to see Margaret and Tony more and more alone. Now I would like to go back to when I think the romance first started and tell of some of the charming, funny, touching and surprisingly often serious moments, which paved the way of Margaret and Tony to their final decision to marry.

There were the many days and evenings they spent alone at Windsor Royal Lodge—the times they drove off together for dinner in Tony's studio-cum-flat in Pimlico—the times he had to ask me to cash him a check to take the Princess out on a spree—their midnight bathing alone—the times Tony happened not to be present when the Queen turned up at Royal Lodge at weekends when they didn't expect her—Tony with Prince Philip in Scotland.

But first of all I would like to tell about the first time I saw this man who was to have such a meteoric rise in society and become the husband of my Princess.

It was on the occasion that the Queen Mother threw one of her popular formal luncheon parties at Clarence House. It was in honor of the High Commissioner for Rhodesia and Nyasaland in July 1959.

The luncheon was held in the huge drawing room on the ground floor of Clarence House—a room hung with gold drapes. Since it was a formal lunch, the table was laid with the Queen Mother's silver gilt dishes and cutlery and I, serving on table, wore my semi-state livery.

I suppose it must have been a rather awe-inspiring occasion for Tony much as it had been for me the first time I had to wait on such a luncheon party.

Bright sunlight streamed in through the four large windows in the room as the guests took their places at the long table. Tony was sitting, his hands clasped together on his lap, on the right hand side of Princess Alexandra. Princess Margaret was four places along to the right of this. The sun was shining full on his face and he kept looking along to his right where Margaret was sitting as if seeking some sort of encouragement. But at the start of the meal Margaret was too much occupied with the other guests to take much notice.

At the time I did not know who he was. But he attracted my attention by the way he was looking around the room at the other guests whom he obviously did not know. And he kept eying me and the other servants in our liveries with a sort of obvious wonder.

None of my fellow servants knew who he was either. I thought he must have some connection with the Commissioner since only important people were invited to these luncheons by the Queen Mother.

My chance to satisfy my curiosity came during the lunch. As I bent over his shoulder to serve him I looked hard at the small name card set at his place. It said simply . . . . Mr. Antony Armstrong-Jones.

He glanced up as I spooned vegetables on his plate and smiled. I was quite shocked. I had come to expect only a stony stare from top people when I served them. Now here was this young man smiling at me in an obvious attempt to be friendly. I wanted to smile back then because I knew he felt out of his depth in that company but I dared not. It was just not done.

During the meal he spent most of the time talking to Princess Alexandra who surprisingly enough treated him like an old friend. I felt I would have to make some enquiries as to who this young man was whom I had never seen but who was on good terms with the Princess.

He spoke in a soft slightly high-pitched voice and with a great deal of gesticulation like the French. Sometimes he even waved his hands across the table to illustrate what he was talking about. This was when he turned to answer questions from Miss Iris Peake who was seated on his right.

As far as I could tell they were shooting questions at him about photography which he appeared to know a great deal about. But he apparently was interspersing his answers with what must have been a series of amusing stories, for he tended to giggle a lot and the Princess and Miss Peake were smiling.

He was wearing a navy blue suit with a white shirt and plum colored tie. His fairish hair was groomed in his characteristic manner, which I thought rather ridiculous then. But I didn't know that one day it would set a new style for men's hair fashions.

During lunch he threw occasional glances along the table in Princess Margaret's direction but she was busily engaged in a conversation with one of the official guests. She looked in his direction only once during lunch and that was when he burst into a fit of loud giggling laughter. Then the look seemed to contain a warning and he was subdued for a few minutes afterwards.

After the meal the guests rose and, led by the Queen Mother, moved off in the direction of the morning room. It was as they filed out of the drawing room that I noticed something funny about Tony's walk. He was stepping along with a strange spring-heeled action.

I watched him carefully as he walked out of the room. His slim figure was emphasized by the tightness of his trousers which tapered away to about sixteen inch bottoms.

In the morning room he was again thrust into the company of Princess Alexandra and Miss Peake and didn't get a chance to talk with Margaret all afternoon. Later I went to the front door and waited for the guests to leave. Finally Mr. Armstrong-Jones appeared. He was one of the last to leave.

He approached me along the corridor and stopped when he came abreast of me. He smiled and said, "I don't think I've seen you before have I?"

"No, sir," I replied. "I don't think you have." This was hardly surprising as it was the first time to my knowledge that he had been invited up to the house.

Then he asked: "What is your name?"

"Payne," I replied.

"Oh, you are John, who is with her Royal Highness," he said. "She has mentioned your name to me. I must say I have always been impressed by the way in which she has spoken of you to me." Then he went on: "She has often told me 'John did this for me today' or 'John did that'. Now I know who she meant. I hope to be seeing a lot more of you in future, John."

"I hope so too, sir," I replied.

"I think you will John," he said, and murmuring goodby he walked down the steps and out across the courtyard. He did not have a car with him that time and walked away through the main gates to the right hand side of the police lodge and I stood and watched him stroll off in the direction of the Mall.

I knew that he was off to the Victoria Palace to photograph the Crazy Gang—one of the Queen's favorite comedy teams.

It was not until some time later that I learned why the young photographer had got on so well with Princess Alexandra. He had seen her on numerous occasions before when he had visited Kensington Palace, which was one day to become his home and that of my Princess, to photograph the Duke of Kent, her mother.

And this was probably the reason why he was first introduced to Margaret. I suspect that Princess Alexandra, pleased with the results of Mr. Armstrong-Jones's work with her own family had felt bound to recommend him to her cousin Margaret, whom she knew was fond of photography.

Over the months I built up a picture of Mr. Armstrong-Jones's past career. His father, Ronald Armstrong-Jones, Q.C., was a successful legal consultant who had divorced Tony's mother and had married twice since.

His mother remarried to the Earl of Ross whose ancestral home, a sprawling castle, is in Offaly, Ireland. Tony was brought up in the castle and the local villagers were very proud of him. After his wedding to Princess Margaret, Tony took his Royal bride to Ross Castle and the couple was mobbed by the cheering villagers.

He had been taught photography by a local druggist and by summer 1959 had built up a sizable business which boomed when it became known that he was taking photographs of Royalty.

And this was the man who was to drive the last cobweb thoughts of Peter Townsend out of my Princess's mind. But despite this, and although I knew the couple was happy, I never really felt happy myself at the match. While Townsend seemed to project force and vigor, Tony was not that type of man. I felt my Princess was wasting herself on this friendly but unsuitable man.

Often I think back to that first day I saw him and how I watched him briskly stepping out along the pavement with his head in the air and a spring in his step and I wish that he had walked away and never returned to claim Margaret's hand in marriage.

Tony seemed perfectly at ease whenever he was in the company of the Queen Mother and often talked to her with his hands tucked deep inside his trouser pockets. I don't think she ever took this to be a sign of disrespect; it was just his usual manner.

This informality was probably due to his experiences with other lesser members of the Royal Family during the previous eighteen months when he had been on the fringe of the Margaret set and was taking photographs of her cousins.

It was really only after Mr. Armstrong-Jones had been coming to Clarence House for some months that I learned through the "grape vine" that he had been a constant escort of Princess Margaret. One who never came to the house. I never found out why all that changed and she started inviting him.

Shortly after the Queen Mother's luncheon party, which was Tony's first visit there, I noticed more and more frequently the initials T.A.J. on Princess Margaret's letters when I went out each morning to collect them from the Lodge. The policeman there had noticed, too, and he asked me, "Who is the Princess's new boy friend?"

"Boy friend?" I replied. And then it set me thinking. I had not thought of Mr. Armstrong-Jones at that time as being anything but an ordinary acquaintance of Margaret's.

But with all the extra letters that were coming in signed with his initials it dawned on me that perhaps here was a replacement for Townsend in my Princess's heart.

Letters from Tony were delivered to the house by hand and

with them often came brown paper packages which usually turned out to contain photographs. In fact it was not unusual in those early days to get two and sometimes even three letters or packets a day.

Princess Margaret never failed to be thrilled by the photographs Tony sent her and often I would hear her asking him for a special one which she knew he had taken but had not included in the bundle sent to her.

Sometimes I saw these brown packages opened in the Princess's sitting room and saw that the photographs were landscapes and portraits of my Princess—quite obviously products of the Armstrong-Jones studio. Margaret kept many of these photographs in a separate album which she would browse through in the evenings when she was alone in her sitting room.

But at this time and throughout their courtship I never once saw a photograph of Tony in Princess Margaret's possession or even in Clarence House.

One thing did strike me though. Even up to the time of her engagement those three tiny portraits of Peter Townsend never left the Princess's bedside table.

It was about a fortnight after the Queen Mother's luncheon party that I saw Tony Armstrong-Jones again. But this time it was in a much more informal setting. A weekend down at Royal Lodge Windsor.

Princess Margaret traveled down to the Lodge in her Rolls-Royce and Tony must have made his way there in his battered shooting brake because he did not join the Royal party for the trip down.

Later when he was more accepted by the Queen Mother, Tony was to spend the weekend alone with Margaret down at Royal Lodge, but for this weekend a party had been made up. On later occasions, too, Margaret chose not to travel down in her own car but to go with Mr. Armstrong-Jones, in the shooting brake.

This weekend I noticed as we prepared to leave the house that Margaret was slightly tensed up. This was to be a great moment for her. Her new escort was to be put in close contact with her mother for more than 36 hours. This was a test for any young woman who wants approval of a new boy friend, but it was even worse for a Princess whose mother was once Queen of England.

For Tony too that weekend must have been something of a strain. If he had flopped with the Queen Mother it could mean his affair with Margaret might come to a very abrupt end.

There were eight people invited to that weekend at Windsor Royal Lodge. They included Tony Armstrong-Jones, Lady Elizabeth Cavendish, Lady in Waiting to the Princess, Lady Elizabeth Bassett, who is Lady in Waiting to the Queen Mother, and Colonel Gilliatt, the Queen Mother's private secretary.

Margaret was there helping to play hostess with her mother. At this first weekend down at Royal Lodge Mr. Armstrong-Jones was valeted by the Queen Mother's personal footman, because it was she who was hostess.

Later it was I who helped Tony over his problems of dress and procedure—and who incidentally explained to him some of the boners he dropped unconsciously in the company of his Royal friends.

After he arrived I did not see very much of Mr. Armstrong-Jones until dinner. He had changed by this time and was looking very smart—something I was to remember at later weekends when he turned up with Margaret and sat down to dinner in sports shirt and slacks.

He found himself the center of conversation during the meal. I noticed that Margaret was doing most of the questioning—possibly to draw him out and indicate to her friends that she wanted them to make a fuss of him. She talked to him mainly about photography and the work he did down at the Pimlico studio.

The Queen Mother surprisingly enough had some very intelligent questions to put about photographic technique—a subject I had previously thought she knew very little about. She also showed a great interest in his theatre design work for which he was at that time fast making a name in London.

During the meal Tony was seated on the right hand side of the Queen Mother who was—as was her privilege—at the head of the table. Margaret was seated some feet away at the other end of the table, which made it difficult for the young couple to have any sort of private conversation. Margaret had to ask all her questions in a half shout, which more or less made it impossible for the other guests to ignore the shy young man who had been thrust among them.

But throughout the meal, and indeed during most of the evening to follow, Tony chatted animatedly and lengthily to the Queen Mother who, for her part, was happy to see someone else do the lion's share of the talking.

I could see by this that Tony had got over his greatest obstacle and had made a hit with the Queen Mother. She seemed to approve of him as a friend to Margaret and of course she had something in common with him because of her great interest in art, design and decor. But I have often wondered since the couple became married whether the Queen Mother would have approved so much of their friendship then if she had known what it was going to lead to later on.

But at the time she seemed satisfied—a fact which obviously pleased Margaret greatly—and for the time being Tony Armstrong-Jones was in Royal favor. But that wasn't to last long.

The following morning after this dinner party I had my first of many experiences of Mr. Armstrong-Jones's bad habits. The first, which earned the disapproval of all the Royal family including Margaret, was his habit of never rising early in the mornings.

On the particular morning it was well past eleven before I saw him wandering down into the lounge. Princess Margaret had already finished her early morning vodka and orange juice and had strolled down to the stables to talk to the head groom about the condition of her horses.

He had gone straight to the lounge and there he remained for nearly three quarters of an hour hunched in a chair, still half asleep, reading the morning newspapers. This finished, he got up slowly and stretched a few times. Then, rubbing his eyes sleepily he went back upstairs to his bedroom. I quite thought that he had decided to go back to bed.

But no, he reappeared a few minutes later with a camera slung over his right shoulder and I watched him lazily idle down the steps and out into the garden which stretches out in front of the Lodge.

I stood out of sight at the window to the lounge and studied him as he pottered from spot to spot in the garden in an aimless sort of way. I presumed he was looking for a suitable subject for his camera. He looked like such an energetic young man in the evenings. But now I was seeing him at his most listless. I was later to learn that Tony never properly woke up before 2 or 3 o'clock in the afternoon.

At about 12:45 the Queen Mother, who had been out in the park for a few hours exercising the dogs, came in and found me still waiting in the lounge. She must have realized that I was watching someone out of the window because she came across and glanced out on to the garden.

She asked me: "Are there any of the guests still in the house, Payne?"

"I believe Mr. Armstrong-Jones is in the garden, Your Majesty," I replied. But I knew that she had already seen him from the window.

"I will go out and join him, then," she said, and after giving me a searching look walked out of the lounge. I turned and saw her come round the corner into my view and with the dogs still in tow go over to Mr. Armstrong-Jones.

He showed her his camera and I saw her nod in answer to one of his questions. Then side by side they moved off to another part of the garden and out of sight. The sun was shining brilliantly and during the next hour I saw them from various windows in the Lodge as I went about my duties. Tony took a number of photographs of the Queen Mother posed against backgrounds of flowers and with her dogs.

Then Princess Margaret came back and joined them. The three of them were enjoying the sunshine and the pleasant relaxation out of the eyes of the public and remained out there for some time—pausing only while Mr. Armstrong-Jones came in to collect another three rolls of film. Then they came in to change and join the other guests for lunch. Margaret's eyes were shining and the Queen Mother was looking at the young couple and smiling.

After lunch and yet another change into lighter clothes, the whole party, including Princess Margaret and the Queen Mother, went out onto the terrace and sat in wicker sun chairs and deck chairs, enjoying the balmy breeze which brought the scent of roses and a thousand varieties of flowers wafting in from the garden.

Some of the company just sat relaxing, half asleep in

the warm sunshine and lulled by the drone of honeyladen bees. A few others were reading, nodding over their books, and I saw Princess Margaret look often in the direction of Tony Armstrong-Jones, who still had a camera slung about his neck.

Every few minutes he would glance up from the magazine which lay open on his lap and look at the Princess. Their eyes would meet and a meaningful smile would pass between them. Then unnoticed by the other members of the party they would return to their reading. My Princess, wearing a light, wide necked summer dress, had already caught the sun, and her face, arms and shoulders had been colored a soft honey brown. Her hair, rippled by the gentle breeze, had never looked more lovely. And she was wearing the minimum of make-up. Later in the months to come I often recalled the tranquil afternoon at Royal Lodge and decided that of the times I have seen them together it must have been then that Tony lost his heart completely to my beautiful Princess.

This then, was the standard sort of family weekend at Royal Lodge which I had seen so often. And in its way it proved the last in a series of similiarly uneventful trips which had gone before. After that I was to witness the more intimate weekends toward the end of the summer, when only Margaret and Tony were present. The stage had been set for love and Cupid had found two willing participants.

On the Wednesday and Thursday of the following week Mr. Armstrong-Jones turned up in his dusty gray Borgward at about 7 o'clock in the evening at Clarence House to take Margaret out. It was on that Thursday that I ushered him along the main corridor and led him to the Princess's sitting room.

Margaret was sitting on a settee reading when he went in. She did not bother to get up but just looked toward us and smiled and murmured: "Oh. Hello Tony."

At this time he did not get the customary escort's kiss or the more familiar "darling" with which the Princess normally greeted her male companions. Tony took her hand and said:

"Good evening, Ma'm."

"Will you serve Mr. Armstrong-Jones with a drink John?" Margaret asked me and motioned for Tony to sit down next to her on the settee. They stayed there for about twenty minutes—the Princess relaxing against the back of the settee, dreamily staring into the small fire and looking lovely in her favorite flame orange tulip style cocktail dress, sipping a whisky and water. I remember that she kept that dress longer than any other.

As I served Mr. Armstrong-Jones with a whisky and dry ginger I heard the Princess tell him of the boring time she had had at the meeting of a society at St. James's Palace that afternoon.

It was a never-ending source of amusement to me to see how Princess Margaret reacted to some of these duties which were thrust upon her from the Palace. Because of her honorary position with some organizations it was a must for her to attend their annual conferences and this usually entailed making a speech.

Quite often she could be thrown into a bad mood by receiving a request from a society asking her to become their honorary president or chairman. And I did not blame her for this attitude. For a lovely and vital young woman like Margaret could have had no real interest in the old fogeys who were responsible for organizing the various big social functions of these societies.

But on this particular afternoon it was blazing hot and Margaret had been enjoying the sunshine until it was time to change to attend the meeting. I heard her tell Mr. Armstrong-Jones how she had walked across the gardens to the Palace in the warm sun.

Then how her pleasure had been spoiled by those horrible bores at the meeting. But Margaret was not always so harsh with her hosts. For any charitable organization she would give up hours of her time and come back with enthusiastic reports about what had taken place in the debates.

When he heard her story of the St. James's Palace ordeal Tony chuckled sympathetically and said: "I would never envy you your task." He little knew that before twelve months had passed he would be sharing the boring routine with her.

The room was softly lit and the couple talked against a background of romantic music from the stereo record player. Tony idly ran his fingers through the Princess's mink stole which was hanging loosely across her bare shoulders. This was Princess Margaret's favorite way of spending the early part of her evenings.

My services were no longer required and the Princess motioned for me to leave. When I left the room they were both leaning back, their hands close together and eyes closed, listening to the music. At about 8 o'clock the bell rang for me and I went along to the sitting room. As I reached the door Princess Margaret and Tony emerged hand in hand and I went ahead of them to the main door.

Tony without thinking climbed into the driving seat leaving my Princess to walk round to the other door by herself. I sprang forward to cover up Mr. Jones's bad manners but Margaret was in gay mood and this breach of etiquette for which she would have cut someone else dead went unnoticed. She just smiled and I stood back, their goodbys ringing in my ears to be drowned in the roar of the exhaust as Mr. Armstrong-Jones drove off.

These first visits set the pattern for the months to come. I was to see the Royal romance develop at Clarence House and in the secluded privacy of Windsor Royal Lodge. After that outing with Tony, Margaret seemed to change. She lost the haunted look which had occasionally come to her eyes in those terrible heart-rending months following her separation from Peter Townsend. Now I was seeing a new Princess, a vivacious, never still, often thoughtful young woman whose beauty grew more splendid with each day.

In the following week Tony Armstrong-Jones called three times at the House. And Margaret in only those few short days since his last visit had changed her way of greeting him. Her eagerness to get to his side was obvious in the way she jumped to her feet as I showed him into the room. Twice they went out alone and un-chaperoned. But the third night—coincidentally it was again a Thursday—the young couple stayed in.

This evening was to be the first of their many visits downstairs to the private Clarence House cinema in the basement. I had left the couple alone in the Princess's sitting room after serving them with drinks. Half an hour later, about 7:30 the Princess called for me and I went in. I knocked before entering. This was not a necessity—servants did not have to knock—but I did it out of respect for my Princess and in the knowledge that she would not wish to be burst in upon while she was alone with Mr. Armstrong-Jones.

They were sitting on the settee as usual. Margaret's right hand was clasped in Tony's left. A Sinatra record was playing softly. As I moved toward them the Princess sat up. Pulling Tony to his feet she turned and told me: "Now John. We would like to go down to the cinema. Is everything ready?"

"Yes—Your Royal Highness," I said.

"Then we shall go down immediately," said Margaret and led Tony out of the door and along the corridor. Outside in the main corridor she took him by the hand and the three of us walked slowly toward the elevator. I got into the lift with them and pressed the basement button. Our footsteps echoed on the stone-flagged basement corridor as we walked—myself a few feet ahead—into the little cinema.

The cinema is really a small hall, intimately lit with soft wall lights and centrally heated. It has a gently sloping floor and can seat about fifty people in armchairs arranged loosely in rows of eight or nine. Unlike the more luxurious arrangements at Buckingham Palace which had been fitted with a wide screen, the cinema at Clarence House had just the normal squared screen which is found in most small cinemas in the country.

When we arrived at the cinema everything had been made ready for the showing of the film "The Wild Ones" ... which had been banned to the general public in the rest of the country. The star was Marlon Brando, one of Princess Margaret's favorite screen heroes. The reason Clarence House was able to show a film which had been banned by the censors was that it had the status of a private club. In Britain a private club can show any type of film without seeking the censor's permission.

The Princess strode to the back of the cinema and sat down in one of the armchairs. She patted the one next to her indicating that she wanted Mr. Armstrong-Jones to sit down there.

I placed a low table by her side and Princess Margaret asked: "Have you got any cigarettes John?"

"Certainly Your Royal Highness," I said and produced a

packet of her favorite brand from my pocket and left them. I always took the precaution of carrying a spare packet with me because I knew Princess Margaret could get terribly irritable without cigarettes.

The Princess told me to tell the projectionist to start the film. So leaving the couple sitting there together I walked from the cinema and went round to the projectionist's room and prepared to watch the film from there. The Princess and Tony sat for an hour and a half in their red plush arm chairs, smoking throughout and cooled by the aircon-ditioning plant. I sat a few feet behind and slightly above them with the projectionist.

I was not able to see the couple from where I was sitting and so sat back and enjoyed the film. For I knew that while my Royal mistress was down there with Mr. Armstrong-Jones I would not be needed upstairs.

At the end of the last reel I got up quickly and for a few moments forgot where I was. Then suddenly realizing that Princess Margaret and Tony would be waiting to be taken back upstairs I rushed round to the cinema entrance and opened the door quietly. To my surprise the couple had not moved. They were sitting in the same positions but now their hands were touching and they were motionless—their heads turned toward each other as they gazed into each other's eyes.

I did not want to interrupt them but I could not have backed out of the cinema again, so I moved forward slowly, gave a slight cough, and with my eyes cast down on the carpet waited for them to move. When I knew they had seen me I raised my head in time to see the Princess release Mr. Armstrong-Jones's hand.

Margaret rose from her armchair and stepped toward me. Then, taking his hand again she drew Mr. Armstrong-Jones near her and motioned for me to lead the way out. They followed me, still hand-in-hand, and we went back to the lift and returned again to the sitting room.

Blinking a little from the unaccustomed light after the dimness in the cinema, I asked Her Royal Highness if she wished anything to be served.

"No thank you, John," she replied. "We have decided to eat out tonight."

"Will you require drinks before you go, Your Royal Highness?" I said.

"No. We will see to those ourselves," said Princess Margaret and I was dismissed.

Arrow points to basement studio where Tony lived during his engagement to Princess Margaret. He did his own cooking in this apartment in London's Pimlico section.

Margaret and Tony stroll arm in arm across the grounds of the Royal Lodge at Windsor.

While the Princess puffs on a cigarette (above), her sister, Queen Elizabeth II, gasps as a mount slips during the Equestrian Olympics at Stockholm. (Below) Margaret clutches her camera as she and Tony study the Horse Trials at Badminton, England.

On May 6, 1960, Princess Margaret took Antony Armstrong-Jones as her husband. The ceremony was in Westminster Abbey.

Models of the Princess and her husband stand side by side, immortalized in wax at Madame Tussaud's waxworks in London.

The Princess and Tony, accompanied by their pets, leave Kings Cross Station after an overnight journey from Scotland. Only a few weeks later, a son was born to the couple.

BLACK STAR

The Queen Mother says goodby to Princess Margaret and the Earl of Snowdon (title conferred by the Queen so her nephew would not be born a commoner) as they left Clarence House, where David Albert Charles Viscount Linley was born, to return to their home in Kensington Palace.

WIDE WORLD

Chapter Eleven

The following day Princess Margaret rose late, proof that Tony Armstrong-Jones had kept her out until well into the early hours. It was a Friday and Mrs. Gordon saw me in the morning and told me that we would be traveling down to Windsor Royal Lodge for the weekend.

I went down ahead of the Princess in the Royal shooting brake—favored by the Queen—driven by one of the Queen Mother's chauffeurs. With me was Chief Inspector Crocker the Princess's personal detective, on loan to her from Scotland Yard, the British Police headquarters in Whitehall.

Margaret's luggage, which for these weekends usually consisted of two large suitcases and her make-up box, was put in the back together with a crate of Malvern water and a few bottles of whisky.

By the time we had unpacked and arranged for dinner it was 6 o'clock. Princess Margaret arrived shortly afterward alone. I was a little puzzled by this, as the house guests normally traveled down with the Princess or arrived very shortly after her.

But time went by and none appeared and I told myself that Margaret must have decided to spend a quiet weekend alone. I took the precaution of asking the Royal Lodge steward if any guests were expected that day and he told me: "No. I haven't been told of any."

At about 7 o'clock the Princess rang for me to go to her in what was known as the Octagonal room. I found her standing in front of one of the windows playing with a lighted cigarette between her fingers. She seemed to be nervous.

She spun around, a hopeful look on her face as I walked

145

in, but seemed disappointed when she saw who it was. "Oh it's only you, John," she murmured. Then looking at her watch: "Has Mr. Armstrong-Jones arrived yet?"

I must have looked blank for a few moments and I tried not to let my surprise show in my voice. I said: "No, Your Royal Highness. I did not know that Mr. Armstrong-Jones was expected this weekend."

"Oh yes, of course he is," snapped back my Princess. She glanced at her watch again and added: "He should be here at any moment. Please go and look for him."

"Certainly Your Royal Highness," I replied, and left her standing there, her eyes flicking from the clock in the room to the watch on her wrist.

I had never seen Princess Margaret so anxious to greet one of her guests before, not even her favorite escorts like Billy Wallace and Dominic Elliott. Tony Armstrong-Jones must even at that time have had quite a strong hold on my Princess's heart for her to worry about his non-appearance as she did.

These thoughts were still going through my mind as I wandered down the corridor to the front door. I opened it and stepped down onto the gravel walk a few paces so that I could see along the drive. I looked in the direction of the main gate but there was no one in sight. I assumed Tony had been held up in the heavy rush hour traffic out of London and was just about to return to the Octagonal room to put this suggestion to the Princess when I heard a telephone bell ringing inside the house.

The Royal Lodge Steward, Mr. Havers, answered the phone before I could get there. I stood by him as he muttered a few curt "Yesses" and "Nos" into the mouthpiece. Then he put down the receiver and turning to me said:

"John. A car with Mr. Armstrong-Jones driving it has just passed through the gates of the park. It will be here in a few moments. Will you go to the front door and meet him?" I went out and stood in the evening sun watching for his car to come into sight around the bend in the drive.

It took him about three minutes to make the journey and he drove up to the house at about 30 miles per hour. He pulled up a few feet from where I was standing with a crunching skid on the gravel driveway. His hair was disarranged and looked very boyish as he sprang lightly from the driving seat and slammed the front door. As he came over to me I stopped him.

"Where is your luggage, sir?" I asked.

"You'll find it somewhere in the back of the car, I think John," he said, jerking his thumb over one shoulder in the direction of the dusty shooting brake.

"Her Royal Highness is in the Octagonal room waiting for you," I told him. "If you wait a few seconds I will show you in to her."

He was dressed in a pair of cavalry twill slacks, a brown sports jacket, striped shirt and sported a red tie with a blue flowered motif. He stood impatiently at the front door hopping from one leg to the other—he found it difficult ever to stand still—while I got his luggage from the car.

I was much astonished to find his luggage consisted of one rather soiled brown zipper holdall. But there was no other article in the car and I assumed this was all he had brought.

I carried it inside and put it down in the hall on a carpet and asked him to follow me into the Octagonal room. He was ahead of me by the time we reached the doorway and I had to almost push him aside to open the door. Princess Margaret did not appear to have moved since I last saw her. She was still standing by the window, which overlooks the gardens, her hands clasped in the typical Royal fashion firmly behind her back.

She could not have heard us enter or thought I was alone for she did not turn around as the door opened. I waited a few moments and when she still did not look around I announced simply: "Mr. Armstrong-Jones, Your Royal Highness." She turned round quickly enough then, a bright smile of pleasure on her lips and walked towards him with arms outstretched. I guessed what was coming next. It was inevitable. Margaret was so relieved to see Tony that all thought of Royal procedure must have been swept from her mind.

As she reached him Tony's arms went up and he caught her fingers in his. Then with their hands held in front of them they leaned towards each other and kissed. It was a tender moment and one which I will never forget. Obviously it was not their first kiss, but it was their first in someone else's presence.

I watched as Tony's arms slowly crept down and around

Princess Margaret's tiny waist and pulled her closer to him. Her fingers, freed from his, caught at the back of his coat and she clung to him.

It was by no means a Royal escort's kiss—those I had seen many times. Rather it was a full-blooded lovers' embrace. Their lips were tight to each other. Indeed it was the same sort of heart-felt embrace which I had seen the Princess offer to only one man before—and that man was Peter Townsend.

Princess Margaret snuggled closer to Tony, and, after what seemed an age to me as I stood by the door, slightly embarrassed, they parted and stepped away from each other, their hands together again. The Princess was the first to break the magic silence of that moment.

"Tony. How wonderful it is to have you here," she said in a half whisper. It was adequate yet inadequate to the situation, but Margaret had at that time no real experience of dealing with the one she loved.

If Margaret's remark was simple Tony's was ridiculous.

"Ma'm, it's delightful to see you again," he replied. Even then after Margaret had made it obvious what he meant to her, Tony could not forget who she was. He could not bring himself to use anything other than the correct form of address when speaking to her.

I almost felt like laughing, so serious was his tone. But Margaret didn't seem to notice. It was enough for her just to have him with her. She had still not changed from the pale blue woolen dress in which she had traveled down to the Lodge.

Leading Tony over to the drink tray Princess Margaret looked over to me and seemed to see me for the first time. With a smile and a nod she dismissed me. Having been brought up to have servants constantly in her presence I had not embarrassed her at all by being there.

I left them there talking over their drinks, Princess Margaret with a cigarette in her hand and Tony perched on the arm of a settee with his drink clasped between the palm of his hands watching her.

The Octagonal room is one of the most pleasant in the Lodge. And it is an ideal setting in summertime for young lovers to meet and plan in the warm afternoons and evenings.

As might be imagined it is an eight sided room, its walls panelled in a light-colored maple wood. It had been

built to the design of George VI, the late King and Mar-
Lodge which owed their existence to his enthusiastic design-
ing. The room is carpeted luxuriously in a thick gray pile and
the curtains are a heavy brocade. Almost diagonally left
when one enters the room is a large French window leading
garet's father. It was just one of the many things at the
out onto the terrace which stretches along that side of the
Lodge. To the right of this are two large windows which
look out over the beautiful sunken rose gardens.

All the furniture in the room is delicately covered in a
soft pink material which has white flower patterns on it. The
Octagonal room was essentially a room to relax in and one
of Princess Margaret's favorite retreats. It had three large
armchairs as well as three settees.

Just to the right of the French windows was a big im-
portant-looking manly desk which had belonged to the late
King but was now used exclusively by the Queen Mother,
his Queen, who jealously guarded it against even her children's use.

Behind the door was a huge imposing brick fireplace with
an iron basket-type grate suspended in it. I have often stood
in front of this fireplace in the colder weather and enjoyed
the warmth thrown out by a banked up log fire and tried
to imagine all the happy scenes that it must have witnessed.
Margaret and the Queen Elizabeth, when they were children,
sitting by the feet of their parents, the King and Queen,
spreading their hands to the blaze and listening to stories of
travel and adventure at sea by their father.

Leaving the couple, I went back to the front door to pick
up Tony's bag and carried it up to the first floor and his bedroom. I placed it on the large double bed and walked
across to the window and pulled back the partly drawn
blinds. It was still quite light outside and I could just see the
brilliant red ball of fire which was the sun above the treetops
of the great park.

Then, anxious to get my chores done quickly, I went over
and unzipped Tony's bag. The sight which met my eyes made
me step back a pace and I stared aghast at the contents.
Everything seemed to have been rolled up in a ball. With
a feeling of great consternation I remembered that Tony
would have to dress for dinner with my Princess within the
hour.

So I looked first for his dinner jacket. I found it screwed up and badly creased at the bottom of the bag. He had brought an evening shirt with him which had obviously been worn before and had not been laundered since.

I looked at the pile of clothes on the bed and set about sorting them out. The rolled up newspaper interested me. I unwrapped it and found a pair of crumpled and worn pajamas marked by the newsprint. He had brought along two extra pairs of shoes—suede bootees and a pair of black patent leather evening shoes. I fished out a leather case which was crammed with toilet gear—after-shave lotion, talc, deodorant and hair cream—and another case with an electric razor in it.

One thing which amused me. I noticed that Mr. Armstrong-Jones favored the same talc and toilet water as myself and later I was to see Princess Margaret give an appreciative sniff whenever I passed close by her.

Down the side of the holdall I discovered a dark gray suit which had been carelessly tossed in, a black bow evening tie, and another ordinary red tie. The whole jumbled mess would have been a disgrace to the average man—but to a man who was to dine with his country's favorite Princess it was worse. It was a sin. Especially as the clothes were well cut and of good material. But it was typical of Mr. Armstrong-Jones attitude, which was slap-dash and lazy at this time. I wondered what his flat and studio could be if they were anything like the state of that bag.

By the time I had sorted out the clothes and put his pajamas under the pillow on his bed I found it was past 7 o'clock. I knew that the couple would be changing for dinner shortly after 8 o'clock and as I had made up my mind I could not allow Tony to appear downstairs to dine with my Princess in such shabby gear I bundled his dinner jacket and evening dress shirt under my arm and took them down to the kitchen.

I pressed his pants, did what I could with his jacket and then studied the creased and stained shirt. I thought of substituting one of my own but it would have been too big on him. There was nothing else to do. I would have to try sponging off the worst marks and iron it dry.

It was 8 o'clock by the time I finished and was reasonably satisfied with the results. I took the clothes upstairs again and laid them out on the bed ready for him to change. Then I walked across to the adjoining bathroom and ran a bath for him. I took one more look about the bedroom and glanced out of the window down onto the main drive and across in the direction of the Royal Chapel. This view of the drive was later to prove invaluable to Tony when the Queen dropped in unexpectedly.

By this time it was twilight so I opened one of the windows. I then swished the curtains together and went downstairs. Princess Margaret and Mr. Armstrong-Jones had already left the Octagonal room by the time I got down and when they rang for me a few minutes later I found them in the lounge.

The couple was standing when I entered and I could see that they were ready to go to their rooms to change for dinner. The Princess was first to speak.

"John would you please put two small tables in here?" she asked. "We have decided to have dinner here so that we can watch television."

"Yes of course, Your Royal Highness," I replied and with a meaning glance at Mr. Armstrong-Jones I said: "I have laid your things out ready for you, sir. They are all in order now." My Princess looked puzzled by this remark and looked at Tony. But he just stammered a thank you and I could see he knew what I meant.

I noticed that during that weekend they did not use the dining room at all. After being dismissed I went and fetched two tables from the landscape room and set them up a few feet away from the television set and spread a cloth over them. Princess Margaret and Mr. Armstrong-Jones had already gone up to change and I quickly tidied the room and emptied the ash trays.

With a few minutes to spare before being required to serve dinner I took the opportunity to wander out through the lounge on to the terrace. It was still quite warm outside and as I looked along the side of the Lodge I saw that most of the rooms were lit up from inside. It was certainly a magnificent country retreat, ideal for entertaining and relaxation and well away from the hustle and bustle of town life.

The Lodge was rather a sprawling building because odd bits had been added from time to time by the late King, who had always felt at ease there. The Octagonal room was

perhaps the most interesting because of its unusual shape. It
was set at the apex of two corridors, one of which leads
to the front door and faces out onto the gardens and terrace
on which I was standing smoking my cigarette.

I often wandered about the Lodge inspecting its cosy rooms
and warm decor and it was in this mood that I turned away
from the terrace and along to the front door.

Just inside the doorway to the right was Princess Margaret's
bedroom which I was never able to enter. To the left of the
door was the Queen Mother's bedroom. There were no other
rooms on the right, but a large table dominated the corridor
and on it stood a mirror.

Often I would see the Princess or the Queen Mother leave
their bedrooms and pause in front of this mirror to pat
their hair into position, check their make-up or just generally straighten themselves up before going along to the
lounge or dining room round the corner in the other corridor.
Margaret, always fussy about her personal appearance, was
often caught smoothing her eyebrows in the mirror even
though she had just spent half an hour doing her make-up
in her bedroom a few feet away.

To the left of the corridor between the Queen Mother's
bedroom and the entrance to the Octagonal room in the corner was a stairway which led up to the guest rooms and the
female staff bedrooms.

Also upstairs was the Royal nursery, which during the weekends I was down there was hardly ever used. Occasionally
when the Queen and Prince Philip came to stay, the Royal
children Prince Charles and Princess Anne would sleep there.
But the room was originally intended for Princess Margaret
and Princess Elizabeth. It was there that the famous Windsor
doll house stood, not as large as the one which stood in the
grounds but big enough for a toddler to climb inside.

Windsor Royal Lodge, after the death of Queen Elizabeth
the Queen Mother, will be passed down to Princess Anne when
her brother Charles succeeds to the throne.

The Lodge was in an almost permanent stage of siege during Margaret's affair with Townsend in the previous years.
Press photographers and reporters had surrounded the
grounds in the hope of catching a glimpse of the couple together. And some of the more daring photographers had actu-

ally hidden in bushes, armed with telescopic lenses in case there should be the chance of a quick snapshot of the pair.

But those days were over. Though I dare say the Press would have swarmed to Windsor if there had been a hint of the romance which was going on down there each weekend.

My mind full of speculations and memories, I turned away from the front door and walked slowly along the corridor and turned right into a much longer passage. I passed by the Octagonal room and the landscape room on the left and re-entered the lounge.

The lounge is by far the biggest room in the Lodge. It is wood panelled for three parts of the way up the walls in a pale green painted wood—another idea from the imaginative mind of King George VI. At the top of these panels the room is ringed with a gay circle of ancient heraldic shields and crests.

A large multi-colored Persian carpet contrasts strongly with the high plain white ceiling. I had entered the room from a door in the right-hand corner which leads onto the corridor. I walked over to the opposite side and drew the curtains on the three large windows—the center one a French window leading out onto the terrace. The terrace runs the full length of that side of the house and catches the sun for the most of the afternoon and evening.

Standing at the French window I glanced to either side of me at the two desks—one the Queen Mother's and the other Princess Margaret's. Then I walked over to the grand piano on my right and lifted the lid idly to let my fingers brush along the keys and listened to the soft cascade of notes. It was here that Margaret spent much of her time when alone—playing and practising. I let the lid close with a bang, went across to the door and paused before a large table against the side wall.

Arranged haphazardly on the table were more than fifty miniature busts of Margaret's ancestors. I fingered a few of them and placed them carefully back in position. Margaret loved those busts and I knew that she would spot if any of them had been moved.

To the left of the door was a big brick fireplace and on either side of this was a settee and an armchair. The furniture was finished in a mixture of dark blue and red. I was about to leave by the corridor exit but changed my mind and walked back across the room to another smaller door in the left-hand wall. In that corner was a screen and behind this the drink tray.

I glanced around once more at the familiar sight of the huge radio and 21-inch television set which stood in a heavy wood cabinet and at the two card tables which I had set up near the fire for the couple's dinner and left the lounge. The door I had chosen opened out into the Landscape room which connected with the Octagonal room.

I did not pause there but went on into the Octagonal room and out into the corridor again. I passed the main dining room and staff sitting room and the pantry on my right and turned at the end of the corridor into the male servants' quarters. This part of the house extends in a wing out on to the garden.

I had spent longer than I had realized in wandering about the house because it was almost time for dinner when I reached my room. I knew I would have to hurry for the Princess did not like being kept waiting. I flung my jacket onto the back of a chair and snatching up my toilet bag, hurried to the servants' bathroom. A quick wash and I was ready to face my Princess again. I put on my jacket, straightened the creases in my trousers and after combing back my hair strode down the corridor past the dining room.

I was just in time. Margaret and Tony were turning the end of the corridor as I reached the lounge door. I opened it for them and as the couple went inside announced that dinner would be served immediately.

The meal had already been prepared and was standing on hot plates in the pantry. I whisked up a napkin and put it over my left arm and carried two bowls of clear consommé through to the lounge.

During dinner the Princess and Tony sat side by side on two pink and white covered Chippendale chairs watching the television. After serving each course I retired from the room without waiting to be dismissed and did as well as I could to guess how long to allow for them to finish each course before going in to clear away the dishes.

The couple seemed to be hungry for they ate a good meal. I remember the grateful look which Mr. Armstrong-Jones cast me while I was clearing away the empty soup bowls. I knew that he was trying to silently thank me for making his dinner jacket presentable. And indeed when on it looked as smart as any I had seen.

There followed generous helpings of roast beef, potatoes, mushrooms and chopped carrots with a fruit salad and fresh cream as a desert. The Princess did not finish her main course but both accepted a glass of brandy each with their coffee.

But later I noticed that Margaret had put hers down untouched on the drink tray behind the screen. I was not really surprised because brandy is not one of my Princess's favorite drinks.

Dinner over, the young couple sat down side by side on a settee in front of the fire which, though not needed for heating the room, added to the cosiness and warmth of the atmosphere.

The television set was still on but neither of them were watching it. The Princess lay back on the settee, her eyes closed and her hands folded in her lap, apparently half asleep. Her yellow satin cocktail dress was ruffled under her and her diamond necklace and earrings flashed and sparkled even in the dim light of the flames from the fire and a single standard lamp.

Tony was leaning forward slightly gazing into the fire, his hands clasped around his knees with one foot resting against Margaret's tiny evening slipper. Princess Margaret held a cigarette holder loosely in her fingers and the smoke curled up almost straight to the ceiling from the glowing end of her cigarette.

Both the steward and I sensed that the couple wanted to be alone for we both hurried to get our job finished. We removed the table-cloth and carried the two card tables back into the Landscape room.

Then I went back once more to the lounge and asked Princess Margaret: "Do you want the television set left on, Your Royal Highness?"

"Yes," she replied. "Leave it please, John. We shall be watching it later."

"Will you require me further this evening Ma'm?" I asked.

"I think so. Yes," said Margaret. "I will ring for you when you are wanted."

This was a sign that I should leave and I went to the servants' sitting room and read a magazine and listened to the radio for two hours. At about 11 o'clock I was summoned to the lounge and as I entered the Princess was switching off the television. Mr. Armstrong-Jones was sitting in exactly the same place as before. In fact, he did not appear to have moved.

Princess Margaret turned to me and said: "You will not be required again tonight John."

"Thank you, Your Royal Highness," I replied, inwardly fuming that I should have been kept from my bed for two hours after being told that I would be needed that night. But it was all in a day's work to me and I put on a good face. After bidding them both good night I went along to my bedroom, leaving them sitting together by the fire.

Although this weekend had been a relaxing one for all of us it produced none of the abandon which was to come at later "runaway weekends" at Royal Lodge.

Margaret must have been planning this weekend for some time and in those forty-eight hours they must have gotten to know each other better than they could have done in a month of normal escort duty.

Here they were free to do as they pleased, completely alone and unchaperoned, to talk about themselves, their experiences and possibly their future.

Was it during this weekend, I wonder, that they first realized that chance had thrown them together for the rest of their lives? Did they at this time consider the opposition that was bound to come from Margaret's sister and from the circle of advisors who must always have wished that Margaret could have made a "tidy" marriage to some English nobleman of their choosing?

Was it during this weekend that Margaret decided that she had learned enough from her experiences of the Townsend affair to be determined not to listen to the arrogant and stifling advice?

They had known each other now for two years but had finally found one another here, in the warmth of a full-blooded kiss.

Life took on a new meaning after that for my Princess. I could not know what she had decided but I do know that from this point she let no one and nothing keep her from being with Tony whenever she chose.

They became inseparable. But in spite of this and the

obvious feelings my Princess had for Mr. Armstrong-Jones I must honestly say that I never approved of him. My earlier impressions of him as a man stayed with me throughout their courtship and even when I watched them enter Westminster Abbey for their marriage I did not feel happy at the match Princess Margaret had made.

Chapter Twelve

The following weekend was to prove an unhappy one for me. For not only did I get a severe reprimand from my Princess but I was soundly taken to task by the Queen herself for an incident which was caused by the stupidity of one of her own servants.

It happened when we moved out of Clarence House toward the end of summer for the traditional holiday at Balmoral Castle in Scotland. Balmoral has always been a favorite spot of the Royal Family of England. The castle is gaunt and huge and dates back to the middle ages. From its turrets and battlements one can see across the rolling countryside to the distant heather-covered hills.

Princess Margaret was in a particularly awkward mood as we left Clarence House for the short drive across London to King's Cross Main Line station where she was to join her own private train. This was partly due, I think, to her separation from Tony for a fortnight.

But to Margaret any journey by train was a trial. She always looked with loathing at the stations she had to visit. For although the red carpet was laid out along the platform for her and she was met with all pomp and ceremony by the top-hatted stationmaster, little was done to disguise the general filth and debris which always litters our railway terminals.

I used to watch her face flinch when she glanced about her, although, thoroughly trained as she was in Royal behavior she never took the smile from her face. On that day the journey across London had taken longer than usual and the Rolls Royce had been held up at nearly every traffic light and road junction on the way. This had not improved my Princess's bad mood.

When we arrived at the station she spent barely seconds in greeting the stationmaster and hurried along the platform to her compartment. The noise and the staleness of the air seemed to depress and anger her for as she climbed aboard the train I heard her say to Mrs. Gordon: "Oh Ruby, these awful stations. They nauseate me."

I could see that my Princess was working herself into a real temper, and this was borne out twenty minutes later when I was called to her sitting room on the train and found her pacing up and down for all the world like an angry she-cat.

Standing there, not daring to speak until spoken to, I noticed that she had spilled the contents of her little traveling bag onto one of the tables and now she scowled at me and snapped:

"Where is it?"

"Where is what, Your Royal Highness?" I said in some trepidation, fearing the worst.

"My book, of course," she fired back at me crossly. "You have forgotten to pack it."

"Oh," I murmured. Then in a flash I remembered the book, a romantic novel which I had left lying on a settee in her sitting room back at Clarence House. I knew she had asked me to make sure I brought it up to her bedroom to be packed.

"Oh . . . Oh . . . is that all you can say?" she fired back at me. "What do you mean Oh?"

"I must have forgotten it. Your Royal Highness," I said, and flinched as she turned on me.

And I thought again of that book lying on the settee and wondered what had made me overlook it. But I was quickly brought back to the present as my little Princess, pacing up and down as she spoke, went on and on. I stood to attention, my face burning.

She was by this time thoroughly aroused and was working off her bad temper on me.

"How could you be so stupid?" she raged furiously. "What am I going to read on my way to Scotland? Do you think I am going to read the timetable?"

"Of course not, Your Royal Highness," I answered obediently.

"Of course not," she mimicked.

There followed a horrible silence as Margaret stopped ranting to fit a cigarette into her holder. I had no defense but I sought to make up to her by some gesture like lighting her cigarette for her.

I fumbled in my pocket for a match, but then came the final humiliation. With a glare and a shrug of irritation, she snatched up a lighter from the table, lit her cigarette and waved a hand towards the door.

"Go away," she shrilled angrily. It was over.

I went away as she had ordered, thoroughly chastened and upset. But I soon got over it. It was typical of my Princess whom I knew so well by now, to find her anger had evaporated when next I came into her presence the following morning.

She was pleasant as ever and asked me where we were and how long it would be before we got to the end of our journey. The incident was over and I never expected to have such a Royal dressing down again.

Alas, I was mistaken. It came much sooner than I could have possibly realized.

Two days after our arrival at Balmoral Castle I was to run into Royal trouble again.—But this time it was my Princess who comforted me.

The incident only happened because I obeyed my order from one of the Queen's servants. It was late in the afternoon. I had taken up my position outside the great castle door as instructed and was enjoying the pleasant sunshine and reflecting on my good fortune at being a servant in the Royal Household.

I was awaiting the arrival of the Queen, Prince Philip and Princess Margaret from the grouse moors after a day's shooting. The Queen's servant had told me that when the car arrived he himself would open the door for the Queen, and I would attend to the other doors.

We took up our positions and waited. They arrived in a huge shooting brake and to my astonishment the Queen was at the wheel. Prince Philip was sitting quietly by her side. They all wore their off-duty shooting dress, the Queen and Princess Margaret with headscarves over their hair and in tweed jackets and pleated skirts, the Prince in his tweeds and heavy boots.

As the car drew up, I went round to the opposite side of the car from the Queen and flung the door open for the Prince. To my great horror—for I was well versed in the ways of Royal precedence—I saw the Queen look round for a moment then open her own door and climb out, her face going pale.

She slammed the door hard and threw a furious glance toward the house. Then, her eyes flashing, she strode around the bonnet of the shooting brake and came right up to me. She paused about two feet away and stood there glaring. The Prince and my Princess had by this time stepped out of the car and were standing close by, watching and silent. They must have known what was coming but at the time neither of them made an effort to control the Queen. I suppose if they had then they too might have been treated to a tongue lashing. As it was, I alone was to bear the brunt of that Royal rage which was welling up inside my Queen.

Seemingly controlling herself with some difficulty the Queen asked me: "Do you know who I am?"

"Yes, Your Majesty," I replied.

"Then kindly remember yourself and your duties in future," she snapped and stormed off into the castle. Once again my face burned under the whiplash of Royal temper and I stood rooted to the spot.

But then there was a touch on my arm. I looked up and saw Prince Philip standing there looking sympathetically at me.

"Never mind," he said. "I'm afraid it is one of Her Majesty's off days." And with Princess Margaret on his arm he strolled towards the house, where the Queen stood tapping one foot on the gravel drive.

"Philip," she called sharply and turned on her heel and went inside.

Later that evening, when I was attending to Margaret, she said suddenly: "You were scolded by Her Majesty today, John. But you mustn't let it upset you."

I was very grateful to hear those words of comfort from my Princess. It was just another example to me of how Margaret looked after the interests of her servants and did not treat them like wooden images, which was my impression of the Queen's attitude.

After we had been at Balmoral for a fortnight, Mr. Tony Armstrong-Jones arrived as a guest of the Queen and I was very pleased for Margaret's sake that he was there, especially after the kindness she had shown me following my brush with the Queen.

I feel sure that he must have been invited on my Princess's suggestion because, as I was to learn in the next few days, he never seemed quite at ease with the very top branch of the Royal family tree. And I knew that the Queen would not go out of her way to be pleasant to someone she did not approve of even if it meant pleasing her own sister.

And although I kept my thoughts to myself it seemed to me at the time significant in view of what I had already seen both at Clarence House and at Windsor Royal Lodge that this man was being drawn by Margaret into gradual acceptance by the rest of her family. But I knew that none of them so much as dreamed just how close had become the relationship between the two. They were in love—that much I knew or strongly suspected—but how soon the news was to be broken and what would be the reaction of the Queen and Prince Philip and even the more sentimental Queen Mother when they learned that Margaret had ideas about marrying a commoner was still a matter of speculation. In the following year I was to see the reaction for myself. Philip and the Queen Mother smiling with happiness as Margaret walked to the altar. The Queen looking unhappy and disapproving throughout the ceremony as these two were joined as man and wife.

But if this holiday at Balmoral was a kind of initiation ceremony for Tony, I am certain that it was a very tough one. It must have been hard for him to get into the swing of things at the castle. After all, the Royal Family are essentially an energetic and sporting family who like nothing better than rising early and dressing in thick clothes and boots, going out onto the moors for a day's hard shooting, riding or walking.

This, of course, was not the kind of thing that Tony had been trained for. He was essentially a town man with charming manners, a pleasant line of conversation and of delicate build. Couple these points together with his late-

rising habit and one has everything the Royal Family dis-
approves of. So my heart went out to this man—even though
he did not have my respect or approval in his courtship of
Margaret.

He made a gallant attempt to keep up with his hostess and
host in their many activities. But he never actually carried
a gun, as did the other gentlemen led by Prince Philip.

Tony would stand awkwardly in the butts, seeing to it if
he could that he never strayed far from the side of Princess
Margaret, who seemed to hold back her usual enthusiasm
for the sports so that there should not be too great a difference between Tony and the others.

In actual fact Tony looked out of place in just about every
place they went except the drawing room. He even looked
different in his dress, although he made what I considered a
first class effort to match them when he joined them on the
moors.

He produced a pair of plus fours—bulky trousers that
lace up tightly just below the knee—and wore them with
knee length thin stockings and suede boots that came up
to his ankles.

This was set off by a loose fitting corduroy jacket and a
sharp peaked cap which he always seemed to wear pulled
well down over his eyes. But I can only say that he invariably looked awkward and very much ill at ease whenever
he wore this uniform.

He only looked like the old Tony I had grown to know at
night, when all the gentlemen changed into dinner jackets
and the ladies wore their evening dresses and jewels. In this
situation he stood out. The men who looked so rugged in
their outdoor costume found it their turn to suffer the feeling
of awkwardness when they found themselves in stiff collars
and bows. Tony on the other hand was relaxed and easy
in this garb. I never found out during that visit if he had
made a better job of packing because one of the Queen's
servants was detailed to valet him. But he looked extremely
smart. Possibly due to good packing but more probably from
the attentions of a skilled valet.

But one thing was spared him in the way of following the
Royal order of dress. Being of Welsh extraction, he was
barred from wearing the Scots kilt, always popular with the

Queen and Margaret. I think Mr. Armstrong-Jones must have been very thankful for that.

But by and large he managed to scrape through somehow and mix in with the other guests and all would have been well if he had not fallen foul of Prince Philip. It was that which put the seal on his misfortunes and very nearly resulted in a row between himself and Prince Philip. Fortunately for all concerned Tony is a peace-loving man and was able to laugh or rather sheepishly grin the episode away.

If there was one single thing which did most to undermine any efforts Tony made to mix into the spirit of the routine, it was his love of bed—or perhaps his loathing of getting up.

He was always the last down to breakfast. The other gentlemen had usually been up some hours before Tony put in an appearance. By that time they had all eaten a full breakfast and were preparing for a day in the countryside. But Tony rarely came down until they had finished and he was left to eat alone. More often than not breakfast for him those mornings was a scrambled affair. He had to bolt his food down so as to catch up with the party. And he never seemed to have time to prepare himself fully for the long day in the open that was to follow.

Many a time the Land Rovers which the Royal party used for transport to the moors for shooting would be waiting outside fifteen or twenty minutes for Tony to join them.

It was after about half a dozen of these late starts on the part of Mr. Armstrong-Jones—I always suspected that he planned to be left behind—that I saw Prince Philip get really angry with him.

The Prince had been sitting at the wheel of his Land Rover with two companions, all anxious to get away, waiting for Tony as usual. He sat patiently for about ten minutes and then he started to give long blasts on the horn every few seconds and appeared to be getting very agitated. At last he turned to one of the guests and snorted in a loud voice:

"Where has that bloody man got to? Still in bed I suppose." And his companions grinned. For to them Tony's late rising was a standing joke. And the Prince's impatience a source of amusement.

"I think he is coming now," one of them said to Philip.

"And about time too," snapped the Prince with a withering look in Tony's direction.

As he spoke, out of the house tumbled Tony, his coat-tails flying and his hat askew on the back of his head. He ran across to the Land Rover and with a stream of apologies falling from his lips clambered over the side of the vehicle. Prince Philip did not reply. Instead he let in the clutch with a jerk which set Tony staggering back into his seat and tore off down the drive after the rest of the party.

Naturally enough I did not follow the Royal party when they went out onto the moors except to help them set up the lean-to marquees under which they had lunch.

These were really quite rough and ready affairs, consisting of cold meals packed in hampers and served out by the ladies of the party. I shall never forget the sight I had of the Queen down on her hands and knees spreading slices of bread with butter and handing them round to the men.

The ladies also packed everything away when the meal was over and neatly done it was, too. I think it made a nice change for them to be able to do the ordinary chores which most women try hard to get out of. The only thing left for the servants to do was carry the hampers back to the castle.

From what observations I could make on the few times I went out with them Tony always appeared to drag along behind Philip and his friends, being only at ease in the company of Princess Margaret.

Indeed she seemed to spend a great deal of her spare time trying to explain to him just what the other men were doing. Apart from this they had plenty of other things to occupy their minds. They both carried cameras wherever they went and spent hours on end taking photographs of the party, the wonderful views across the Scottish highlands and moors, and of each other.

The ten days of his visit went by all too soon for my Princess and it seemed no time at all before she was waving goodby to him as he was driven down to the railway station. She was a sadder Princess after his departure but cheered up when packets began to arrive for her from London. I found out that they contained hundreds of prints—some of them photographs he had taken and some which had been snapped by Princess Margaret. She spent the rest of her holiday showing them to her friends with obvious delight.

But before he left I noticed that Tony was never really accepted by the higher members of the Royal Family. After dinner in the evenings it was the custom for the whole family and all their guests to gather in the drawing room where the Queen and Margaret organized games. Or sometimes they would sit around the fire and talk and sip their drinks and stay up far into the night, all sense of time completely gone. And there were times when the records would spin on the player and the couples would set off and dance and dance and dance until I thought they would never stop.

I was very often in and out of the drawing room serving drinks and seeing to the guests and Princess Margaret. I remember how Tony used to stand on the fringe of the circle near Philip, smiling and nodding as required by the conversation, but taking very little active part in the arguments and debates that were going on.

This would have been difficult even if he had wished to do so for the conversation was always dominated by Philip's booming voice. The Princess did her best to try and draw him into the flow, by changing the subject to one she knew he was familiar with or asking him a direct question, but Prince Philip somehow managed to brush him aside and stop him before he had a chance to get properly started.

This antagonistic attitude of Philip's towards Tony was not caused only by the differences over Tony's late rising. I feel sure there was something else, something much stronger behind it. It is a well known fact that Phince Philip has always been particularly fond of Princess Margaret and never loses an opportunity to talk to her or help her in and out of a car or onto a horse. He was there whenever she needed someone and they shared a similar sense of humor.

But if Philip had a knife out for him Tony did not appear to take offense. At least not openly. If he was not a hit with the gentlemen, with the ladies Tony was quite at home. When he left he was seen off by the Queen, the Queen Mother, and of course Princess Margaret. Between the Princess and Tony there was only a handshake when they parted, none of the affection which they had displayed in more intimate surroundings.

And with a wave and a smile to all off went Tony on the

fifty-mile journey to Aberdeen to catch the London train, with a packed lunch of chicken provided by the household in his baggage.

Thereafter my Princess stayed on at Balmoral castle for another five weeks and life there went on in the same round of shooting, hunting and strenuous open-air life which the Royal Family loves.

My Princess, like all the other ladies at the castle, including the Queen and the Queen Mother, abandoned her dress sense completely and wore whichever old thick tweeds she could find. To me she looked absolutely terrible in the big, floppy hats—they called them "pea-picking" hats—which were favored by the ladies for their daily excursions.

Margaret used to spend a lot of time up in her suite of rooms at Balmoral, writing letters and pasting up the photographs that she and Tony had taken there.

I have since thought that that holiday at Balmoral would have been a perfect opportunity, had she already decided to marry Tony, for my Princess to have broken the news of her engagement. She missed him very much after he went back to London and I often found her looking wistfully at the photographs of him in her album.

The days seemed to drag more than ever during the last fortnight of our holiday and I could see that Margaret was fretting to get back to Clarence House and the busy night life of London which she loves so much. After Tony went back the Duke of Edinburgh spent a great deal more time with Margaret trying to cheer her up and make her laugh.

Perhaps he, of any of them, would have been prepared to give her guidance if she had broached the subject of marriage with Tony, since nothing was too much trouble for Philip if it concerned his "little sister".

But remembering his attitude toward Tony during the ten day visit he may have been biased and upset her even more. So she had to be content with her photographs and memories in the knowledge that they would not be parted for very much longer.

Then at last came the time to return to London and home. As usual we traveled in Margaret's own train. That train was more luxuriously furnished than many homes I have been in. It was made up of two converted carriages coupled to the end of a normal service train. They were sumptuously furnished and carpeted throughout in a rich thick pile. Margaret had her own bedroom and dining room and there was a tiled bathroom. Quarters were also laid on for Mrs. Gordon and myself.

Back in London Tony was anxiously awaiting my Princess's return. They met again constantly and hardly an evening went by that he did not call at Clarence House to see her.

They went more and more on trips away together, often to Royal Lodge and there followed some of the most hilarious, romantic, intimate and fascinating weekends I have ever spent in my life.

Everything seemed to happen to us in those next few months. At times I thought that we had experienced everything possible. Then something new would crop up to shake me even more and I would tell myself that it was not really a Royal Princess I was working for.

There was the astonishing time that Tony stood up Margaret for dinner . . . and that was really something.

It happened down at Royal Lodge one weekend. It was blazing hot and rather stifling and Margaret was in none too good a mood. It was shortly after Tony had been accepted into the Royal circle. But even he, although he was on intimate terms with my Princess, could not pass off easily what took place down there that day.

I was sitting reading in the servants' sitting room opposite the lounge when I heard a bell ringing. I put down my book on the coffee table next to the armchair I had been using and pulled on my jacket. Then I hurried across the corridor into the lounge.

Margaret was standing at the open French windows looking out across the gardens. She turned as I went in and said: "Oh, come in, John. I just wanted to tell you to set up two tables in the dining room. We shall be eating in there tonight."

"Yes Ma'm," I replied. "Whom shall I expect for dinner?"

"Why Mr. Armstrong-Jones, of course," said Margaret with a smile. "Bring me the menu and I will choose the dishes."

I took her in a suggested menu and she ticked off the dishes which took her fancy.

"When shall I expect Mr. Armstrong-Jones to arrive, Ma'm?" I inquired, for by this time it was nearly 7:30.

It was well past his usual time of arrival and the question seemed to annoy Princess Margaret. She looked down at the tiny gold watch on her wrist and pursed her lips for a few seconds.

"Never mind John," she said shortly. "Just see to it that his room is ready and dinner is served at 8:30."

"Yes, Your Royal Highness," I replied and left the room.

But 8 o'clock came and went and I began to anticipate trouble. Quarter past eight found me pacing backward and forward outside the main door looking down the drive, expecting and hoping to see Mr. Armstrong-Jones big gray shooting brake race down towards me.

It did not—and for the first time the thought entered my head, what if he's stood her up? It was unthinkable. No one had dared ever do such a thing to my Princess before. But it began to look as if Tony had set a precedent. I wondered what she was doing inside and I was soon to find out. At 8:20 I was summoned to the lounge where I found a thoroughly vexed Princess puffing angrily on a cigarette and scowling at the door. I entered with a queer sort of shiver running through my scalp. I knew that if Mr. Armstrong-Jones did not turn up it was I who was to suffer the Princess's temper.

She moved forward as I entered and said: "Have there been any telephone calls?" I knew what she meant but, of course, Mr. Armstrong-Jones had not telephoned.

"No Ma'm I'm afraid not," I told her. She stood in a lovely snug fitting cocktail dress leaning on the back of a settee tapping one tiny foot on the floor, a sure sign that her temper was near to boiling point.

Then she seemed to come to some decision. "Very well," she snapped. "I shall dine alone."

"Yes Ma'm," I said, and moved off in the direction of the dining room.

"Come back here. Where are you going? I have not dismissed you yet." I knew that Margaret must be very angry to talk to me like that. Although I was just a servant I was usually quite thoughtful in the way she spoke to me.

"I am going to the dining room to prepare your dinner," I told her.

"No you are not," she flashed back. "Fetch a table in

here." Then she added: "If I must eat alone then I will eat in comfort."

"Yes Ma'm," I replied and left the room. As I set up a small table in the lounge near the flickering fire I hoped that the telephone would ring. But it did not and I could see the Princess getting angrier and angrier.

I went to the dining room and removed the ready laid cutlery and carried it to the lounge. I set a place and put out a napkin for Margaret who was standing brooding in a corner of the room staring down at the keyboard of the grand piano and nervously flicking the ash from the end of her cigarette.

I thought of suggesting to her that Mr. Armstrong-Jones may have been held up by traffic or was ill at home or might possibly have met with an accident. But I could not imagine any of these suggestions would help matters so I kept silent.

At 8:30 there was still no word from Mr. Armstrong-Jones and Margaret, her face set in a scowl of disappointment and rage, sat down to eat. But her appetite, as could be expected, had vanished and she just picked at her food, turning away dish after dish with a curt wave of her hand.

Finally to my great relief the meal was over and I began to breathe more easily. The awaited explosion had not come. I began to think that perhaps Princess Margaret had managed to get her temper under control. It had been the most tense experience of waiting at table I had ever encountered.

After clearing away the dishes I went over to the drink tray. I knew that if I got through the next few minutes without an incident then I would be dismissed and probably miss the almost inevitable tongue lashing which I was sure was bound to come.

But I was sadly mistaken. And it was all my own fault. I must have let my nervousness get the better of me because as I went to pour a whisky into her glass the stopper of the decanter slipped through my fingers and dropped with a clatter on to the tray and shattered the silence.

Margaret sprang round, her eyes flashing. Here was something that she could use as an excuse to work off her fury.

"Stop making such a din," she snapped, her knuckles showing white where she clenched a tiny fist on her cigarette holder. "You are always making a clatter. Try and make less noise in future when you are in here. It is absolutely disgraceful."

As she stormed on I adopted my usual stance at rigid attention. It was all I could do. I knew that this was not my real Princess speaking and so tried to let her words pass over me. I thought of the harsh words I would like to have said to Mr. Armstrong-Jones if I could have got him to myself for a few moments. I was furious with him for upsetting my Princess so.

"I'm sorry, Your Royal Highness," was all I could think of to say.

"It is no use being sorry after the act," she scolded. "Don't let it happen again."

As I left the room she said in a quieter voice: "Let me know the moment there is a telephone call for me, will you John?"

"Of course, Your Royal Highness," I said and quickly marched out into the corridor, thankful to be out of reach of her Royal fury.

As I walked along the corridor I heard the shrill note of a telephone ringing. I almost ran to answer it. As I had hoped it was Mr. Armstrong-Jones.

"Could I speak to Her Royal Highness?" he asked in a gay voice.

"She has been expecting you to call her all evening," I told him in my coldest tones.

"Oh dear," I heard him murmur in a more sober voice. Then, "Put me through to Her Royal Highness immediately then, will you?"

I did as I was asked and waited until I heard Margaret's voice on the extension. She said simply: "Margaret." And I put down the receiver.

It was half an hour later when I heard the telephone give a single short ring, the signal that Margaret's conversation with him was ended. I could guess what had gone on during that half hour and imagined Tony's futile excuses being knocked aside by Margaret as she gave him a dressing down. He would not be so eager to forget a date with my Royal mistress in the future I thought, and in a way pitied him for being in such a vulnerable position. He could not very well answer back when the woman who was scolding him was a Princess of the Royal blood. Margaret stayed in the lounge for the rest of the evening and I heard the sound of music wafting out into the corridor from time to time. She must have been playing the piano.

Thankfully, I did not see the Princess again until about 10 o'clock, when she rang. She was still in rather a sullen mood and she told me snappishly: "I shall be riding in the morning. Tell the stables to prepare my horse."

I knew that at this time of night, the horses would be bedded down and the stable boys departed and in their beds. I tried to put this point to Margaret saying: "I'll try to get the stable lads on the phone Ma'm." But Margaret was adamant.

"Make sure I have a horse in the morning," she said. I might have known that to try and reason with her in her present mood was impossible.

I tried the stables in Windsor on the phone but got no reply. So I had to call the head groom from his bed to take the message.

"It's much too late," he said. "You really ought to give us notice before tea time the previous day if she wants a horse." I felt so shattered by now that I was in no mood to argue with him.

"Do you want me to tell the Princess that?" I asked.

"Good Lord no," said the groom. "There will be a horse ready."

And sure enough on the dot at 9:30 the next morning both Margaret and the horse were ready, freshly groomed and prepared for the ride.

Margaret walked briskly down the gravel path, tripped lightly up the two little steps she used to mount the beast, threw herself into the saddle and galloped off. . . .

Chapter Thirteen

That my Princess could be contrary I knew full well, as she had proved to me on many occasions. But the incident which spotlighted it best was the time she came back from Communion at the Royal Chapel to the lodge at Windsor early one Sunday morning.

Princess Margaret has always been a great church-goer and this particular morning she had risen very early to go to the first Communion, and returned just as the other people at the Lodge were finishing breakfast.

Now it was a well-known fact that Margaret never took a cooked breakfast, except on rare occasions when she was away as a guest at the home of one of her friends.

On this Sunday morning I waited for her to return with her breakfast of fruit, China tea and orange juice ready on a tray in the kitchen. On her return she rang from the lounge and I hurried along, not sure where I should serve her breakfast. When I entered she was staring out of the window idly patting her hair, having taken off her little hat.

It had been slightly chilly that morning and the journey through the park had brought color into her cheeks and she looked rather like an impish fairy—and from her looks was obviously in a bright mood.

"John," she said turning around, "will you bring me my breakfast?"

"Yes, Your Royal Highness," I replied cheerfully. "I have prepared your usual breakfast on a tray. I will bring it straight in."

"But I want a proper breakfast. Poached eggs or something. You know I always have a proper breakfast after church."

I was amazed. It just wasn't true. But nevertheless if that was what she wanted that was what she would be given. So I said I would bring her poached eggs.

"With coffee," she added as I reached the door. And I wondered what she was up to.

I went straight to the kitchen but the cook had already packed up and disappeared. So I set to and prepared the meal myself. By 9:15 this breakfast of eggs, toast and hot coffee had been prepared and I carried it into the lounge. I set it down on a table and stood the coffepot on the heater. This was nearby on another table.

Margaret sat down and lifted the silver dish covers over her plates and sniffed uninterestedly at the food underneath.

I was furious with my Princess for her contrariness. And now, after I had prepared the food myself, she looked as if she didn't want it.

Unfortunately I was tired that morning after a late night and my temper began to bubble up inside me. However, controlling myself, I set out her coffee cup and lifted the percolator from the hot plate prepared to pour her a cupful.

"Don't you think I can do that for myself, John?" she asked innocently. I froze for a second or two and closed my eyes.

"Yes, Your Royal Highness, I am sure you could," I replied and slammed the coffee percolator down on the table with such force that some of the dark brown brew splashed over the lip and over the wall, causing a seeping stain which trickled its way down to the floor. But I did not care. I was just too angry.

"Why, John," said Margaret, with just a hint of teasing in her voice. "Are you angry?"

"No Ma'm," I replied with all the sarcasm I thought prudent. "It just splashed a little. I can assure you it was only an accident."

"Well, I believe you are," she said, a faint smile creasing the corners of her mouth.

"I am not Ma'm," I replied again shortly.

"Well, never mind," said the Princess. "You had better leave me now to get on with my breakfast." And glad to get out of the room, I left.

I could feel my stomach tremble and my lips were pursed and I knew that I had very nearly lost my temper and let fly at Princess Margaret.

But gradually I felt my anger seep away and began to see the funny side of the situation. It was not often that Margaret included me in her jokes and I suppose this incident proved that she thought of me more highly than I had ever thought would be possible.

What a long way I had come since that sunny morning a year ago when I first walked into Margaret's sitting room and talked to my Princess. How frightened I had felt then. How keenly I had awaited news from Lord Adam Gordon that I had been engaged as Margaret's personal footman.

It was with these thoughts in my mind—little dreaming that my service with Margaret would come soon to an end —that I returned to the lounge half an hour later to clear away the breakfast dishes.

Margaret was sitting at her desk, writing. Her breakfast completely untouched except for one slice of buttered toast, stood on the table.

All my anger flooded back. Out of the corner of my eye I saw her turn to watch me as, with face set, I cleared away the still warm eggs, the toast and the percolator of hot coffee. I was mad.

"What's the matter, John?"

"Oh it's just that you haven't touched your breakfast Ma'm," I said.

"No I didn't feel like it when I got it, I'm afraid," she tried to explain. But then with a flash of inspiration or sheer devilment she went on: "You have it instead." And waited to see my reaction.

"No Your Royal Highness. I have already had my breakfast," I said.

"Well, have another one," she insisted, playing the joke out to the bitter end and I sensed, deriving a great deal of amusement out of it.

"No thank you Ma'm." Silence. Then. . . .

"What time did you have your breakfast?" She was not going to give in that easily.

"7 o'clock, Your Royal Highness. I was up early this morning," again with sarcasm in my voice. But she was feeling playful still and after a pause she came up with another attack.

"Well, it's only . . ." she looked at her watch. "10 now. "I'm sure you could eat it."

"Thank you, Ma'am," I said sweetly. "It is just that I don't want another one."

I waited, expecting her to come back with yet another question. But the silence dragged on and it did not materialize.

By this time, smiling quite openly, she gave a shrug and gave up the verbal fence. I clattered the dishes as much as I could on the way out but she just carried on with her writing and the smile stayed fixed.

Actually when I got the tray back to the kitchen I did eat the breakfast. Which proves only that I can be as contrary as my Princess—and get away with it.

It was a breakfast again which involved me in a row with Mr. Armstrong-Jones. But this time I did the ticking off. It came about after a slanging match between Mr. Armstrong-Jones and the cook at Windsor Royal Lodge. I was the go-between.

Really it began on the previous evening—a Friday. Mr. Armstrong-Jones had traveled down to Windsor Royal Lodge in his shooting brake with the Princess by his side, which had become the habit for the couple by this time.

I saw Mr. Armstrong-Jones to his room and later served the couple dinner in the lounge. They spent the rest of the evening watching television and talking. I was in the servants' sitting room when at about 11 o'clock the bell rang and I went in to the lounge. The room was in semi-darkness, lit only by the light from the television and a single standard lamp.

The couple was sitting in the settee with their backs to the door. They had their heads together. Tony's was resting against Margaret's thick curls. And as I moved further into the room I saw that they were holding hands.

"Do switch off the television," said Margaret without looking up.

"Certainly Your Royal Highness," I replied and went across and flipped off the switch.

I stood waiting in the center of the room with my hands held loosely at my sides looking down at my shoes. I was embarrassed to see my Princess cuddling up to Mr. Armstrong-Jones. But finally they straightened up and Margaret looked up at me.

"I want you to take up a breakfast tray to Mr. Armstrong-

Jones's bedroom at 10 o'clock in the morning John," said Princess Margaret.

"Yes. I will see to it Ma'm," I told her.

"You can leave us now John. We will not be needing you again tonight."

As I left the room Margaret got up and walked across to the phonograph. I saw her take a long playing record out of its sheath and put it on the turntable. It was the music from *Oklahoma,* the musical which had been running a few months before in the West End.

I heard the soft tones of the melody coming from the room as I walked down the corridor to the servants quarters, and guessed that they would be dancing. Actually I found out from the police guard, who patrols the gardens at night, that the music had still been going at 2 o'clock the next morning when he made his rounds.

I rose at 7 o'clock as usual the next morning and after doing the early chores went along to the kitchen and collected a tray with Mr. Armstrong-Jones's breakfast from the cook and went up to his bedroom.

Holding the tray in one hand I pushed open the door and had to grope for the light switch because the room was in darkness. The light on, I saw that the curtains were still tightly closed and as usual all the windows were shut tight and latched.

This was normal procedure for Tony, who never slept with his windows open even in midsummer. It was a habit he would soon have to change when he married Margaret, a typical Royal fresh air fiend.

I drew the curtains right back and opened two of the windows wide. Then, setting down the tray on a bedside table, I gave Mr. Armstrong-Jones a shake. Trying to wake Mr. Armstrong-Jones at any time before midday was always a struggle and I had to shove him violently before he showed signs of waking up.

He turned over and slowly opened his eyes, closing them again when he saw the bright light streaming in through the windows.

"What do you want?" he asked testily.

I knew he had been late getting to bed and ignored his gruff comment.

"I've brought your breakfast as the Princess ordered last night sir," I said.

"Oh have you," he groaned, obviously not having heard correctly what I said. "Well I don't remember ordering any breakfast."

"No sir," I repeated patiently. "It was Her Royal Highness who gave the order."

"Did she," he grunted, turned over, pulled the bedclothes over his head and was silent. What was I to do? I knew the Princess would blame me if he was not up by the time she came back. But there was nothing I could do without causing a scene.

So I left the tray where it was and went downstairs. I busied myself about the lounge for the next two hours, tidying up the records which the couple had left scattered on the carpet about the phonograph. At about 12 o'clock I heard a bell ringing.

I looked at the board in the servants' hall and saw it was the bell in the main guest bedroom, the one in which Mr. Armstrong-Jones was sleeping.

When I went in he was lounging back in bed, the top half of his bare body—he never wore pajamas if he could help it—uncovered.

"I want breakfast immediately," he snapped.

"You have had one breakfast already today, and you have let that get cold," I told him equally snappishly, annoyed that he should talk to me in such a tone.

"Do as you are told and bring me another breakfast," he said sharply, looking up and glaring at me through his red sleep-filled eyes.

"Yes, sir," I replied, and took the untouched tray from the bedside table down to the kitchen, where I knew there would be a lot of explaining to do to the cook who was none too fond of Mr. Armstrong-Jones late-rising habits, which always threw her carefully arranged timetables into disorder, and had more than once brought from her a few well chosen adjectives in description of the Princess's guest.

The first person I saw when I got downstairs was the Princess herself. She looked refreshed and happy after her early morning ride.

"Is Mr. Armstrong-Jones up yet?" she asked. This is it, I thought to myself.

"No Ma'm," I replied. "He seems to be rather tired. I am just taking him up another breakfast."

"Another breakfast," she said in some surprise. "Has he had one already?"

"Yes Ma'm," I told her. "But he let it get cold." I thought she would be angry. But instead she found the whole incident amusing.

"He must be very tired then," she smiled, and walked off towards the lounge.

When I reached the kitchen the cook had already started preparing lunch. I told her that another breakfast was needed for Mr. Armstrong-Jones. Something must have upset cook earlier because now she turned on me and in a bad temper said:

"Breakfast. What, at this time of day?"

"Yes," I told her. "He had rather a late night."

"Well you can go and tell him I'm cooking lunch now and if he's too lazy to eat his first breakfast he can go with ut as far as I'm concerned. I'm not going to start preparing another breakfast at this time of day for anyone," she scowled ferociously at me.

"Do you really want me to go and tell him that?" I asked.

"Yes I do," snapped the cook.

So I went back to Mr. Armstrong-Jones's bedroom and told him exactly—without leaving anything out—just what the cook had said.

"Oh did she say that?" he asked in a vexed tone.

"Yes. I'm afraid she did sir," I told him.

"We'll see about that," he snapped and kicked the bed-clothes off him. I heard him muttering about his breakfast and the cook as I carefully laid out his clothes.

"*That* to the cook," he said.

I was rather shocked. It was not gentlemanly at all. And apart from that I thought the cook was quite within her rights to say what she did.

"Please, sir. Remember who you are . . . and why you are here," I told him.

He looked a bit taken aback and then said:

"Oh very well. But I do not think it is at all right that I should be treated this way."

I watched him dress and he did not speak to me again that morning. I went down ahead of him and told the cook about his reaction. She seemed highly amused and we decided that perhaps in future he would be more willing to get up in the mornings.

But we were sadly mistaken in thinking that a little thing like that could persuade Mr. Armstrong-Jones to leave his bed one second before he had to.

After all even the raging of Prince Philip had not had any effect. So what could we expect?

Chapter Fourteen

I loved those weekends at Royal Lodge. In that hot and glorious summer of 1959, prolonged by a wonderful Indian summer well into September and October, I was grateful to have the chance to get away from London's heat and dust for a cool two days at Windsor. There, the air hung heavy with the scent of a thousand flowers from the spacious, well-kept gardens and the mornings, fresh and sparkling, made it seem really worth being alive.

Then, as the year wore on, those runaway weekends with Margaret and Tony became more and more frequent. Almost every Thursday, I anticipated my orders to prepare for another weekend at the Lodge with my Princess. And as they spent more and more time together, I found myself inevitably drawn closer and closer into the web of their slowly entwining lives.

Their happiness, their abandon of the everyday cares of their lives and their disregard for what they must have known would be a difficult time ahead—when their romance became known not only to the Royal Family but to the rest of the world—was obvious to me.

It was ironic then, that on one of those idyllic weekends I should witness for the first and only time, my Princess in a state of white-faced, supercharged Regal fury which was terrible to see.

It was triggered by a disastrous gaffe which Tony made in the presence of Her Royal Highness.

Only the evening before, he and Margaret had been dancing barefoot on the soft carpets of Royal Lodge lounge, to the strains of romantic music from the record player. They danced softly and silently, no sound except the music and the occasional clink of glasses coming from behind the closed door. They had danced until well after midnight, for I turned in at about 1 o'clock and they were still up.

The following day—it was a Monday—we were all making our preparations, rather reluctantly, to return to London. Mid-morning, at about the time Tony was getting up, Margaret rang for me and I went to the lounge to answer her summons.

At first, I did not see her in the room. Then, from behind one of the settees in the corner of the room, her voice came: "Over here, John."

I walked across and found the Princess sitting cross-legged on the floor with a couple of dozen of her favorite records spread out on the floor around her.

"John, I'm sorting out some records to take back with me to London," she explained when I appeared. "If you will wait a moment, I would like you to help me carry them out."

I said: "Certainly, Your Royal Highness," and squatted on my haunches next to her while she sorted through the discs. She was in a wonderfully happy frame of mind and she picked up each record, looked at the cover and hummed a snatch or two of some of the songs.

She picked out a Sinatra long-player and with a wry smile, said: "Hmm, we can't leave Frankie behind can we?' and she put it on the pile she was taking with her.

I picked up the pile and waited with her as she placed one or two more in my arms. Then she said: "Right, I think they will do for now. Take them out and I'll just have a quick look through the rest."

I hoisted myself up, leaving her to her pleasant task and started to walk out of the room.

I suppose I was halfway across the room when the door burst open with a crash and in breezed Tony. When he saw me, he threw his arms in the air and cried: "John, I've been looking everywhere for you. Be a darling, will you, and . . ."

Tony had apparently not seen that the Princess was still sitting on the floor behind the settee. And I could do nothing to stop him from greeting me in this breezy way—as if she were miles away.

But something of the alarm I felt must have shown on my face, for he stopped short, the smile fading from his lips. I felt, rather than heard, the rustle of Margaret's dress as she jumped up from the floor. I said nothing, but saw Tony's eyes widen as we both turned towards the far side of the room.

The Princess was staring at Tony, obviously not pleased.

"What on earth do you mean?" she asked Tony. "Whom are you talking to?"

Tony was discomfited by this cool interrogation. I too was uncomfortable at being a party to what amounted to their first quarrel.

"Oh . . . er . . . Ma'm?" Tony stammered at last. "I had no idea . . . I didn't see you. I wanted John for something."

"And what do you mean by 'darling'?" asked Margaret fiercely, ignoring my presence.

"It's an expression used often in the theatre world, ma'm," Tony said. "I'm afraid I have picked it up . . ." He trailed off

It was some time before my Princess came down to earth the sentence with the ghost of a smile, tentative and humorless.

Margaret regarded him coldly for what seemed half an hour, while the three of us stood tensely still. It was Margaret who broke the silence.

"You may go," she said, looking at me frostily, her chin jutting out, her fist clenched at her sides. I bowed my head to her, glanced at Tony and left the room. Nothing was said while I walked out and closed the door behind me.

When I got outside, I found myself soaked with perspiration. Sweat trickled down the fingers which had been holding the records and I felt its prickly sting down my back. Seeing Margaret like that had been an awful experience.

sufficiently to address me in the friendly tones to which I had grown accustomed.

I do not know how Tony fared. He drove Margaret back to Clarence House that same afternoon in his car, as had already been arranged, and that evening they dined there together. Tony appeared to work overtime at keeping the conversation going that night, but I sensed that Margaret had not yet forgiven him.

But for me, as I say, life with Margaret returned to normal soon enough and life at Clarence House went along as always.

And it was during the following week that I witnessed one of the most moving incidents I ever knew.

Though not a word was spoken, it left me much moved

and the effect of that day's happening has stuck firmly in my mind to this moment.

I have already mentioned that hanging on the wall in the corridor near the front door of Clarence House is a full length framed portrait of the late King George VI.

It was the only reminder of Margaret's father on view in the house. I had passed it a hundred times and had sometimes stopped to look at the impression of that lean, kindly-looking man. Yet I had never heard his name mentioned throughout my stay at Clarence House with the Princess and the Queen Mother.

However, on this particular day, I was hurrying along on some errand for Margaret when I chanced on this moving scene.

I turned the corner of the main corridor and the passage-way leading to Margaret's sitting room with nothing particular in my mind. But what I saw stopped me dead in my stride.

There, standing motionless in the center of the corridor was the Queen Mother. Her hands were clasped in front of her and she was gazing up at the painting of her late husband with a sad, half-wistful smile on her face.

The small strip light above the picture was turned on and the King seemed almost to be looking down from the wall to meet the tender look in the eyes of the Queen Mother below.

I felt it was wrong for me to be there, intruding on the thoughts of Her Majesty. I hoped she had not heard me and thought of tip-toeing away.

But she had heard, and the spell was broken.

With a last lingering look at the portrait, the Queen Mother reached forward and clicked off the light. She turned and walked down the corridor toward me and passed without a word.

I stood where I was until she had passed out of sight, then I walked the dozen or so paces to where she had been standing and looked up at the painting. Now its air of life had vanished, but as I gazed at it, I wondered what the Queen Mother had been thinking. Of their younger, courting days? Of the way her husband had become King almost by accident through the abdication of his brother Edward? Of their years in London during the war? Of his fight against ill-health in the later years?

Filled now with a feeling of some sadness, I turned and, my errand forgotten, returned to my room.

I never saw the light on above the painting again.

Perhaps it was the Queen Mother's own memories of her younger days with her late husband that brought about her tacit acceptance of her daughter's romance with Mr. Armstrong-Jones. She obviously knew that Margaret and he were spending every available weekend down at Royal Lodge, since she herself traveled down there less and less often. And although Margaret was strong-willed enough to have "gone it alone" with Tony, I do not think she would have flouted her mother had Her Majesty frowned on these runaway weekends.

At the same time, I don't think she could have realized all the antics of the young couple during their Windsor weekends.

For instance, I am not at all sure she would have quite approved of the sudden decisions to change from evening clothes to swim suits for a midnight plunge in the Royal Lodge swimming pool, or of the smoochy tempo of some of the dances which Her Royal Highness engaged in with Tony during some of those hot, sultry nights.

Typical of their off-the-cuff decisions was the Saturday night when they vanished without a word and I discovered they had crept out of the house to go swimming in the moonlight. It was just after midnight when I missed them.

I had left them about an hour earlier, dancing to Latin American music, with a full tray of drinks, plenty of cigarettes and a little tray of nuts and crisps to nibble. But when I went over to the lounge to make my final check that they would not need me again. I was mildly surprised to find the room in darkness.

The door was standing wide open and, although it was comparatively early for them to retire for the night, I presumed that they had in fact gone up to their bedrooms. I switched on the lights and went in to clear up. I was busying myself collecting the glasses and ashtrays onto my tray when I was stopped by a sudden peal of laughter, coming it seemed, from the garden. It was the tinkling tones of my Princess.

A little mystified, I went out to the terrace through the French windows to have a look. There was no one in sight, but I stood for a few moments to accustom my eyes to the darkness after the lights indoors.

I nearly jumped from my skin when a figure loomed suddenly close at hand from the shadows of the house. It was one of the detectives whose job it was to patrol the grounds night and day on watch for intruders and he recognized me immediately.

When I had recovered from my surprise, I asked him: "Is there anyone in the garden? I thought I heard the Princess out here."

"They're skylarking in the pool," he answered, jerking his thumb across to where the swimming pool lay. He smiled in a kindly, affectionate way and added: "They're making a night of it, too, by the looks of things."

On hearing this, I shrugged, said my goodnights to the detective, and retired, knowing full well that the Princess would certainly not need me again that night.

The following morning, I happened to meet this policeman again and he was most amused to tell me that he had seen the glow of cigarettes coming from the lean-to shelter at the end of the pool until 3 o'clock in the morning.

It had been a lovely hot night that previous night. I remembered having rolled and turned in my own bed throughout the night in the heat of my bedroom and I did not blame them one bit for staying in the open.

Both Margaret and Tony were good swimmers and during their frequent daytime excursions to the pool, I had watched them often playing happily in the water, pulling each other under, splashing and having little races across the pool. One of their favorite games was to push one another into the water, and when Tony caught Margaret unaware, she would give a little scream and after splashing her way out of the pool, chase him with a towel. When she managed to shove Tony in, she used to stand with her hands on her hips shaking with laughter to see him struggling.

Standing in the sun, her tanned skin glistening with water, my Princess looked absolutely adorable—fresh and full of life and good health. Her supple figure was shown off to its best advantage in the sort of swimsuit she invariably wore. Her favorite was a brief yellow bikini two-piece affair with a halter strap around the neck.

I remember very clearly the first time I saw Margaret so

scantily dressed. It was at a previous weekend at the Lodge when the sun shone hotly, the flowers were bursting in full bloom and the air hummed with the buzz of overworked bees. I had just come in from sunning myself briefly in the garden, when the buzzer in the pantry rang urgently. It showed that I was required in the Octagonal room.

Hurriedly buttoning my tunic, I trotted up. On opening the door, I gaped.

There stood the Princess, wearing only the revealing bikini and a white towel draped loosely around her shoulders. Her body glistened and little droplets of water trickled down from her arms and legs, and I could see the damp print of her footmarks on the carpet from the open windows to the center of the room.

I was too astonished to speak. I simply stood and looked, my eyes taking her in from head to toe. And she stood watching me look, her hands on her hips and a pleased smile on her lips.

Our eyes met and I felt my cheeks burn with embarrassment, but she smiled more broadly than ever.

"It's all right, John," she said. "I have just nipped in from the pool to ask you to bring out a tea tray at 5 o'clock."

"Certainly, Your Royal Highness," I answered. I felt at the same time awkward and in some way flattered that I had reached a point of intimacy with this Royal Princess which made her capable of standing before me, covered only in the briefest clothing that the law permitted without any apparent embarrassment—on her part, anyway. I flatter myself that so complete was our relationship that only to me did she ever show such a complete abandonment of her Royal pedestal. No other servant could have been given that accolade.

Margaret did not move when I answered her, but stood quite still, apparently enjoying the situation. It was one of her playful moods. Then she spoke.

"Will you please bring the wicker garden chairs down to the pool with you when you come?"

And she turned to saunter out of the French windows, a lovely sight to behold, her trim figure silhouetted against the brightness of the sunshine outside.

I watched her go before following her out onto the ter-Then I went over to the shed where they kept a jumble of race, feeling the heat drench me through my thick uniform.

garden chairs, hammocks, tents and so forth and picked out
the two wicker garden seats. To get to the pool, I had to return to the terrace, walk down into the sunken rose garden—
and what a lovely experience it was to step through those
thick clusters of sweet-smelling blooms—before turning right
along a grass path hedged up to shoulder height, going straight
out to the pool itself.

The pool was fairly large for a private swimming bath,
being about fifty feet long—plenty of room for two to play
in. It was surrounded by a narrow concrete path and outside
this, a deep waist of lush turf lawn. I carried the chair past
the springboard jutting out over the deeper end nearest the
house and went on towards the shallow end, where a concrete
shelter with plain duckboard seating had been erected.

I stood the chair on the right-hand lawn, near the lovely
miniature thatched cottage—the dolls' house presented to the
Queen when she was the little Princess Elizabeth by the
people of Wales. Here, Elizabeth and Margaret used to spend
many happy hours, I imagined, when they were brought to
Royal Lodge by the King and Queen.

It was completely and minutely furnished with every item
one would find in a home, even down to little pots and pans
and kitchen equipment. I myself was fascinated enough to
bend myself double and enter the little front door for a look
round the first time I saw it.

Naturally enough, it was the focal point of interest for the
latest little Princess, the Princess Anne, whenever she was
brought there by the Queen or Prince Philip. Prince Charles
too, was not above playing in it with his sister.

I had seen them often enough when the Family came over,
perhaps from Windsor Castle to call on Margaret, but as a
rule, I had little to do with the Royal children.

But there was one occasion when I brushed with little
Charles. It was the time I lost my temper with him and
very nearly landed myself in hot water.

It happened at Sandringham, the Queen's huge rambling
estate in Norfolk, the home where, traditionally, the Royal
Family gathered for Christmas. But it was occasionally used
for long weekends during the summer, when the Queen holds
a flower show and throws the grounds open to the public. At
such a weekend, Margaret had joined her sister, and I went
too.

I had to serve the Queen herself at such times, along with the other members of the household who were her personal servants, and so it happened that on this particular day, I had been told to post myself on the front door and await Her Majesty's return by car from the old market town of Kings Lynn, where she traditionally spent an afternoon shopping, to the delight of the local people.

Accordingly, I stationed myself on the front steps and alerted myself for the sound of the Royal Rolls-Royce arriving.

I had been there for no more than a minute, when I spotted Prince Charles peeping furtively around the corner of the main hallway of the house. Out of the corner of my eye, I noticed him sidle round the corner and hide behind a curtain drape. I thought no more of it, and dismissed his antics as part of some mysterious boy's game of cops and robbers.

I stood in the sunlight, perfectly happily dreaming about nothing in particular when suddenly the back of my neck was stabbed with a jet of icy cold water.

At the same time, a peal of high-pitched childish laughter sounded behind my back. I swung around angrily and saw Charles standing there behind me with a dripping water pistol in his hand.

I muttered a mild epithet, and fished out a handkerchief to mop the back of my neck, feeling at the same time the icy trickle of water down my spine.

"What did you say?" piped Charles, the water pistol disappearing behind his dungarees. The gleam in his eyes flashed a danger warning to me.

"Oh, it's all right, Your Royal Highness," I said, making the effort to stifle my anger. "It doesn't matter." But it was too late.

"I heard what you said," crowed Charles, dancing in delight. "I shall tell Granny"—he meant the Queen Mother —"the moment she comes in."

Then he ran off down the corridor, apparently to refill his water pistol, for a few minutes later, he reappeared and started squirting water at the lights, on the walls and over the carpets, curtains and tables and chairs.

In the few minutes before the Royal car came into sight I pondered on the incident. I had not had very much experience with the little Prince and his ways. I wondered whether he would indeed tell his Granny and whether his complaint would be followed by a dressing-down or worse.

In some trepidation, I watched the car draw up. By this time, Charles had also come out onto the front steps and before I could move, he had run out towards the car. The water pistol had by this time, vanished.

I got to the car in time to help the Queen Mother, who had accompanied the Queen, from the car. Immediately, Charles tugged at her skirts and stretched up to whisper in her ear as she leaned, smiling, to listen. I saw them both look at me when he had finished. But to my utter astonishment and considerable relief, the Queen Mother cast me a sympathetic smile.

She whispered something back to the Prince before patting his head and saying: "Now run along, Charles."

With a haughty backward glance at me, Charles skipped off into the house.

And I never heard a mention of the incident from anyone again.

Although it was a pleasant change to go up to the beautiful rambling house at Sandringham, to walk through the miles of rhodedendrons and stroll on the acres of lawns, I was relieved to get back to Clarence House, to the routine and the people that I knew so much better.

In London during that long, warm autumn and during the idyllic weekends at Windsor I saw the Princess and Tony growing more and more deeply involved with each other. By this time, Armstrong-Jones was Margaret's constant companion. It was he who took her to the theatre, he who escorted her to parties, who was the guest at dinner in the house.

The other escorts—the faithful Billy Wallace, Dominic Elliott and Lord Plunkett—were being slowly discarded. They still received their customary kiss when they called, but they did not call so often now.

On the other hand, it was "Tony darling" whenever Armstrong-Jones called. And he always got a kiss—but more often than not, it was a lingering kiss full on the lips.

He managed to call at Clarence House even when he was not engaged to see my Princess. Many is the time he would turn up unexpectedly and I would hurry along to show him to the Princess's sitting room, only to have him say confidentially: "I'm not coming in today, John. Her Royal Highness is probably busy. Just give her this for me, will you?" And he would hand me a letter or one of the larger envelopes in which he used to deliver photographic prints.

He never waited for a reply to his notes. Often a letter with the initials "TAJ" in the bottom left-hand corner would be delivered through the post in the morning, to be followed by another, delivered by him in the afternoon. Sometimes he even followed this up with a visit in the evening.

It began to happen at this time too, that when he called in the evening, they would not go out. They settled in the sitting room, sprawled on a settee, often holding hands, and relaxed to the sound of soft music. They talked dreamily, murmuring their occasional comments as the long evenings drew a slowly gathering mantle of darkness around them. It has happened that I called into the sitting room and found it quite dark, their presence marked only by the red glow of Margaret's cigarette. Then they would have the lights put on, blinking in the sudden brightness.

Never a day passed without a note or a call from Tony to the Princess.

Yet although I did not recognize it at first, one aspect of his frequent calls was to cause me considerable embarrassment.

Although it happened several times, I can recall the first occasion on which Mr. Armstrong-Jones came up to me with a somewhat apologetic air and asked: "Can you get a check cashed for me?"

And I had to turn down the request because it simply could not be done—although I don't blame Tony for trying in the least. It must have been very expensive indeed, even for a successful photographer, to take my Princess out night after night, send her flowers and drive her about in his car.

His chance to ask me arose one afternoon when he arrived unexpectedly at Clarence House with an envelope full of photographic prints for the Princess. Although he often called on her with pictures on days when he was not taking her out that evening, it struck me as a little odd that he should turn up at this time because I knew full well that they were engaged to go out that night. He could have brought them with him at 7 if he had chosen to.

The real object of his call became apparent when he drew me to one side as we walked back from the sitting room where he had surprised Margaret.

He took a quick, almost furtive look round, saw no one and whispered: "John, what are the chances of cashing a check here?"

And he reached tentatively to the inside pocket of his sports jacket as he spoke.

He looked almost as embarrassed as I felt, but I could only reply: "I'm afraid I have no money, sir." But I added: "Just a moment, I'll go over and speak to the steward, if you like."

Tony nodded eagerly and I left him in the main corridor while I went along to the steward's office and told Mr. Kemp what Tony wanted. But Mr. Kemp pursed his lips and shook his head slowly.

"No?" I queried.

"No," he said. "Oh dear, no."

I accepted that and hurried back to the corridor where Tony stood, understandably ill at ease, glancing continually down the side corridor in case Margaret should come out and ask what on earth he wanted. In his agitation, he did a characteristic little jig from one foot to the other.

He looked up at me hopefully, but I'm afraid I must have looked glum and the light of hope in his eyes faded slowly. He shook his head disbelievingly.

"No?"

"No, I'm afraid not, sir," I said. And to soften what was quite plainly a blow to him, I said something about the office being shut, or the safe being locked.

Tony reflected for a moment, staring at the floor. Suddenly, he brightened.

"Oh well, he sighed. "There's always the pub." And he trotted out of the house and climbed into his car. But once he got in, another thought struck him. He got out and almost ran into the house.

"Of course, you won't tell Her Royal Highness about this, will you John?"

"Indeed no, sir," I reassured him. He seemed satisfied with this and he turned again and trudged out of the door. However, he proved irrepressible in this respect, for he asked me the same thing on more than one other occasion and each time I went into the steward's office—and each time got the same sad reply.

But Tony need not have worried about the opinion of the steward. Nothing could shake the steward's resolve. Not even had he heard the strange conversation, as I did, between Margaret and one of her Ladies in Waiting about a month later.

It must have been about six months before the eventual marriage—when Tony and Margaret must have already agreed on their engagement date—that I heard this.

There was a luncheon party held in Clarence House, a reception for some member of the Royal circle. I was waiting at table during lunch and my Princess was sitting next to the Lady in Waiting, Lady Elizabeth Cavendish.

Lunch was going well. Margaret was, as usual, doing more than her share to make the conversation flow and all around her the burble of conversation was continuous. It so happened that I was hovering around behind Margaret's chair ready to serve her with the main course of the meal, when I heard Lady Elizabeth lean over casually to the Princess and say softly: "Have you heard the news, Ma'm?"

Margaret had been looking down the table and she barely turned her head as she said idly: "News? What news?"

"Why, Ma'm, that your dear cousin Pamela is to marry that Mr. Hicks."

Margaret's fork dropped with a clatter on her plate.

"Oh no," she exclaimed. "She couldn't. Does she realize what he is?"

Margaret was obviously horrified to learn that her cousin Lady Pamela Mountbatten, daughter of Earl Mountbatten, was likely to become the wife of Mr. David Hicks, a well-known interior designer and a home decor expert patronized by some of the rich and fashionable men and women in London.

I don't think Margaret knew him, for I never saw him at Clarence House, but from the tone of her voice, she knew something about him which she didn't like. That, allied to the fact that Hicks was comparatively unknown in Royal circles, may have been responsible for her outburst.

Lady Elizabeth plainly enjoyed the reaction which her

words had produced in Margaret, and she went on: "It's true, Ma'm. After all, they are two of a kind."

Margaret scowled, prodding her almost-empty hors d'oeuvres plate with her fork.

"I really must remember," she said slowly, "to have a word with Pamela before this goes any further."

And she said it with such seriousness and determination that there was a short embarrassed silence at the table, broken by some bright remark by Margaret herself about a play she had seen shortly before. The new topic was seized on by everyone and within half a minute, everything seemed forgotten.

Whether or not Margaret ever did have those words with Lady Pamela Mountbatten, I never knew, but it was obvious that even if she did, she could do nothing to prevent the marriage, for Lady Pamela is now Mrs. David Hicks.

I thought that Margaret's remarks were a trifle odd, considering that at the time they were uttered, she herself must have already made up her mind that she was going to marry a man who would not be received with universal acclaim as the most suitable husband for her.

It is a fact that when the engagement between the Princess and the photographer was announced, there was a great deal of headshaking among the so-called society people of Britain and among that periphery of Court advisers and experts picked from the top families of the country, there was a good deal of downright opposition.

And at the very top, the Queen herself was never happy about it.

I think that there can be little doubt that there was a final showdown between the sisters when Margaret's intentions became clear, and even when my Princess insisted on going ahead with her romance and marrying Tony in defiance of the Queen and the others, her sister found it difficult to forgive Margaret for it.

I have already remarked in earlier chapters how reluctantly the Queen and Prince Philip accepted Tony into their entourage at Balmoral. And that was before they could be sure that the affair between my Princess and Armstrong-Jones would develop into anything serious.

Small wonder then, that Tony took care not to come into

too close contact with his future sister-in-law . . . that he did, in fact, practically hide whenever the Queen called in at Royal Lodge occasionally when she herself was staying at Windsor Castle.

Chapter Fifteen

Tony's habit of dodging the Queen made it quite clear to me that I, in my privileged position as Margaret's constant companion, knew far more about her impending decision than did anyone else. Their runaway weekends, once occasional, became regular. But still they remained discreet affairs and both Margaret and Tony must have agreed that the least known and said about them, the better.

As a consequence, when the Queen was expected at Royal Lodge, Tony would stay up in his bedroom, keeping well out of the way.

Whether by luck or design, the room which he always used overlooked the drive and, further down, the Royal Chapel, to which the Queen and Prince Philip always drove on Sunday mornings. And after church, they very often dropped by for a sherry with Margaret, whom they had met, of course, at the Chapel.

The position of Tony's window was a great advantage to him. He was able to look out and see the Royal cars approaching and he made sure that while the Princess was doing the entertaining, the guest of the house—the only guest, in fact, —remained firmly out of sight.

Nothing he or Margaret ever did or said suggested outwardly that his comings and goings were deliberate, but it was more than coincidence that within a minute of the Royal party's departure, Tony would saunter down the stairs and join the Princess again.

And they would have a drink together and perhaps stroll out into the garden as if nothing had happened.

One of Margaret's favorite habits was to stroll around the gardens. She loved nothing more than to walk slowly through the flowers, stooping to smell them at frequent intervals, admiring the roses and looking closely at the multitude of sweet-smelling and highly colored plants that had been planted in abundance throughout the grounds.

But there was one habit Margaret had that constituted a running feud between herself and the proud gardeners in the Household.

Being an essentially active person, just walking and looking would often prove of too little interest and she would go to one of the potting sheds on the grounds and "borrow" a pair of pruning shears. Armed with these, she marched about, purposefully inspecting the bushes and trees—just as if she was reviewing a guard of honor—until she found something worthy of her attentions. Perhaps it was a bush which had spread a little too much for her liking, or a tree with a branch which could conceivably brush the head of anyone who passed underneath it.

Then, having located her target, she would begin to hack away with the shears. I used to watch her sometimes from the windows of the house, all alone and hacking away like mad and leaving a pile of little clippings on the grass.

Any old plant might be selected for the Royal crew-cut and I smiled to watch her deliberately walk underneath an out-of-the-way tree just to see if she could find an excuse to chop off a low twig or two.

But one day, she went too far. And I can recall it very clearly for it was one of those times when I laughed so long and so much that I hurt my insides. I ached to see my Princess re-planning the garden layout.

I was watching from one of the upstairs windows of Royal Lodge and saw Margaret standing with her hands on her hips, staring at the hedge with divided the rose garden from the lawns adjacent to the swimming pool. I thought at first that she had found a bird's nest or something.

But she turned away from them so decisively that I had an idea that she would be up to her old trick quite soon. So I stayed looking out over the garden, and sure enough she soon reappeared, this time with a pair of workmanlike hedge shears in her hand.

She walked up and down the hedge two or three times, frowning as she did so. She had evidently decided that the hedge was too long and indeed it did necessitate walking right down one side and up the other to get to the lawns on the other side.

It was, I'm afraid, a beautifully groomed hedge, kept by the tender care of the meticulous gardeners in perfect shape the whole year round. But that was before my Princess hit on her brainwave. For the next twenty minutes, my sides ached at the sight of that little figure tackling the man-sized job of cutting a hole out of the hedge with such utterly feminine determination.

She snipped and hacked, chopped and pulled at the hedge until she was calf-deep in a pile of severed branches. She worked away with fierce concentration until she was done, before stepping back through the debris to survey her work.

By that time, the hedge had a wide, ragged hole in it— a wonderful short-cut to the lawn but something which would undoubtedly make the Royal Lodge gardeners shudder. She had to call them, of course, to take away the barrowload of hedge she had removed. I spoke to one of them later in the day and it seemed that in fact he did have cause to grumble.

"It isn't only the hedge," he said sadly. "You should have seen the shed. We found the place looking as if a tornado had hit it." It seems they had been horrified to find their orderly little shed strewn with rakes, spades, forks and other tools, cast aside by the Princess in her search for the shears.

No, I'm sorry to say that the gardeners did not share my amusement at the refreshing sight of Margaret at work.

But I must admit that their grievance was aggravated quite often by Margaret's almost obsessive concern about the state of the swimming pool. It was the gardeners' job to drain the pool every time Margaret returned to London and to fill it again with clean warm water the following weekend in readiness for her next visit.

But once, very soon after she had changed and gone out to the pool one Saturday, she came back into the house with an expression of pained outrage on her face. She asked me to have the gardeners brought to see her at the pool. I was out there too, arranging a trayful of drinks, when the two duty men arrived, prepared, from the look on their faces, for a dressing-down from my Princess.

And they got it.

"Look at that," she said, pointing into the pool. "Filthy. Take a look."

The unfortunate two peered over the edge, looked at Margaret and then down into the water again. Unable to resist, I too, took a discreet peep into the pool to see what it was that had aroused Margaret's ire. Two leaves! Two autumn leaves floating in the pool.

One of the gardeners scooped them out and then they went away. But still the Princess was not satisfied. Ten minutes later, I returned to the pool and found Tony Armstrong-Jones alone, lounging in a garden chair by the edge of the pool. Where was Margaret? Even as I asked myself, she trotted into sight, a stiff long-handled scrubbing brush in her hand.

And without further ado, she started scrubbing the whole length of the pool around the water line quite oblivious of the ironic situation—here was a Royal Princess doing her own scrubbing.

But those weekends, besides being full of romance, were always filled with incidents like this. And without doubt, the craziest scene I ever witnessed was the time that Tony and Margaret decided to take a few snapshots of each other.

I found them quite by accident because I happened to go into the lounge to do a bit of tidying up when I heard a gust of prolonged laughter coming from the terrace. Margaret was obviously enjoying herself hugely at whatever she was doing. And the laughter as it came in through the open French windows was so infectious that I found myself smiling in anticipation as I walked across the room to see if I could share the joke.

I hesitated a moment, but my curiosity got the better of me and I walked out onto the terrace just as another roar of laughter, this time from Tony, burst into the air.

And there, one of the most crazy scenes I ever expect to see, greeted my eyes. Tony and Margaret were taking pictures of each other.

My Princess stood in the sun wearing a pair of old gray man's slacks, a red checked shirt, a pair of black men's shoes several sizes too large. She had tucked her dark curls into a battered brown trilby hat which was pulled down rakishly over one eye.

She was contorting herself to maintain a manly expression

of sternness on her pretty face and leaned nonchalantly against the balcony with a cigarette in her fingers. Beside her was her camera.

But if Margaret looked odd, even odder was the garb into which Tony Armstrong-Jones had crammed himself.

For the purpose of the picture, he was dressed as a woman, wearing some of Margaret's clothes. A camera hung from his neck.

As my eyes roved over him, Margaret began to lose control and she shook with silent laughter before burying her head in her hands and giving herself away to sobs of helpless mirth.

And no wonder. Tony's very male legs protruded from beneath the hem of one of Margaret's skirts—a brown pleated job—and he had rolled his trousers up above his knees. He had pulled on one of Margaret's white long-sleeved nylon blouses and on his head he wore one of her huge floppy picture hats at a ridiculous angle. Finally, he had crammed his feet into a pair of her delicate open laced sandals.

Margaret lifted her head and once again faced the camera. While he fiddled with the mechanism, her eyes caught me standing in the doorway. I shuffled as if about to turn back into the house, but Margaret pulled a face, inviting me to share the joke. I grinned back at her and watched Tony, still oblivious with his viewfinder.

It was about thirty seconds before he looked up, giggling. Then he spotted me. He shot a surprised glance at Margaret and said: "Oh, John, it's you."

Margaret, still chuckling, asked: "Did you really want me, John?" I had no answer, of course, and said simply: "I was just taking a breath of fresh air, Ma'am."

"That's all right," she said sweetly. "You did not intrude." She looked over at Tony, smiling still and he too, saw the joke and started laughing. I bowed my head and retreated back into the lounge. There, I had to sink into one of the armchairs and allow the laughter I had been bottling up over the crazy masquerade to come forth.

I have heard a good deal of rather bitter talk about Margaret and Tony since their engagement and subsequent marriage—some of it suggesting that Margaret took Tony as her husband on the rebound from Townsend or just to spite the Royal Family who had forced her to give up one man and may have wanted to arrange something more suitable for the most eligible Princess in the world.

But if that couple was not genuinely happy, genuinely in love and completely absorbed in each other, then I must have been blind or mad during the time I saw them together. To me, there could be no doubt about the depth of the Princess's affection for Tony. I had seen her at close quarters with most of the people who, at one time or another, had been mentioned as her possible future husbands and never did I see any of them manage to light the eyes of my lovely Princess as did the sight of Tony in these later days.

Back in London, they continued their gay yet discreet way.

But although they went often to the theatre and met the subsequent publicity, they tended more and more to amuse themselves alone, either at Clarence House or at Tony's studio-cum-flat in the Pimlico-road, a district of London which is noted for its cosmopolitan residents. Tony's place was a converted shop at Number 20, next door to a large block of tenement-type flats with an old-fashioned pub opposite at which he used to drink.

By now, Tony's name was mentioned frequently enough in the papers. But he was doing a great deal of photographic work for them and was being hailed as one of the finest theatrical photographers in the country. When he was noted as a member of Margaret's party at some theatre or other, they merely mentioned the fact and recorded it as . . . "also in the party was the photographer Mr. Antony Armstrong-Jones . . ."

It must have amused them both to see how the papers —usually so quick to hitch Margaret to anyone seen out with her more than twice—had passed over Tony so completely. But this suited their plans perfectly, I am sure.

Even in normal circumstances, Margaret did not always enjoy the publicity which followed her everywhere. When she went to the theatre, she sometimes tried to avoid it by booking her seats through a Lady in Waiting. But even so, it happened often enough that the news did leak—and sometimes it made Margaret quite furious.

And one night, after what had obviously been a bit of

a melee among the photographers outside the theatre, she swept into Clarence House, taut-faced and furious. She slammed straight out of her car and marched into the sitting room where she rang for me and, with a foot tapping dangerously, told me to fetch her own detective, Chief Inspector Crocker.

Crocker had been with the Royal party which had gone to see the Brendan Behan play "The Hostage," and had been a helpless witness to the pushing and shoving.

Apparently when she reached her car, Margaret had been surrounded with cameramen who crowded round the car windows, flashguns popping endlessly. So enraged was the Princess that she had, quite uncharacteristically, put her hand over her face to prevent them getting another picture of her.

When I brought Crocker into the room, Margaret was still boiling with anger.

"You'll have to be more careful or make better arrangements when I go out," she started immediately. "Quite obviously these theatre people know you and expect to see me when you arrive. You really will have to do something about it. I can't have scenes like that whenever I go out for an evening."

Poor Crocker! He could do nothing but agree. I suspect that Crocker took the blame for something he could do nothing to prevent, since I imagine that it was the theatre manager or one of the theatre's publicity people who had tipped off the papers.

Thousands of pictures of the Princess appeared in the papers all over the world every year but, being a woman, she had a pretty poor opinion, I think, of most of them. I often heard her pass a remark to Iris Peake or one of the other Ladies in Waiting at lunch about how awful she looked in the papers that morning, asking resignedly: "Couldn't they have used a better one than that?"

My previous employer, of course, had been Lord Rothermere, owner of the *Daily Mail* and the *Daily Sketch,* both of which used extensive coverage of the Princess's movements day by day. But once when I was with her, she held out a copy of the *Daily Mail* to one of the women with a look of disgust on her face.

"Look at that," she said, indicating a picture of herself.

"Isn't it terrible? That's that man Rothermere on the war-path again."

It amused me intensely to hear this reference to my former employer and I suppressed a little smile at the thought of Rothermere's face had he been able to overhear it.

Anyway, the press could only intrude on the more formal occasion and, as I have said, it was the intimate evening alone that appealed more and more to the Princess and Tony. They did the simple things like watching television, dancing together in her room to the music of her records —or going to his flat for the evening.

This struck me as possibly the most startling departure from the rigidity of Royal protocol. In retrospect, it was like a theme from a film—the beautiful Princess, sought after by the most noble Princes, running out for the evening for a simple supper at the humble home of a commoner.

I often wonder how Tony had managed to suggest to Margaret that she come round to his place for the evening, in return for the hospitality she had shown him so often. But however he managed it, there is little doubt that she accepted his invitation with eagerness, for she gave the appearance of complete bliss when they left together for one of these evenings.

At first, I was mystified by the brown paper bags full of groceries that Tony started bringing with him to Clarence House. It struck me as odd that he should bring his shopping with him, and even odder when he told me cheerfully: "Fetch up the groceries, will you John?" as he raced up the steps. And I carried them into the sitting room behind him and put them on a table.

Then I put two and two together. Tony's groceries were in fact their menu for the evening.

Later on, this became part of the regular routine for eating at Pimlico-road and when Tony came and I brought in the paper bag, Margaret would dive in eagerly, asking what he had brought. They would wait only as long as it took to drink a cocktail or two and then they would be away in Tony's car.

I saw them off with the same dignity as if they were going to a State banquet, but I used to imagine them driving the mile or so to Pimlico, letting themselves in unobserved and shutting the door on the world outside.

Did Margaret help with the cooking? Lend a hand with the washing up? Wait on the man she loved? I liked to think she did.

It would not have been out of character for this lovely young Princess to have done this, for although she was aware of her position—all her training had been aimed at making her aware of it—she never abused it. Unlike some other households in the Royal Family and their endless relatives, Margaret's servants were all treated well, not like serfs. And as it was with her staff, so it was with the people she met outside. Although she often mimicked them and privately punctured their pomposity, she always respected them for what they were and what they were doing. Thus, I am sure, Margaret would have in no way stood on her dignity while dining alone with Tony.

Seeing them off for the evening was like seeing off a couple of carefree children to a picnic. They dined well but simply, I knew, since I often peeped into the shopping bag and saw, a couple of packets of frozen food, steaks, perhaps a few slices of smoked salmon and a bottle of wine.

It was about this time that the Princess and Tony accepted an invitation to spend a weekend with Mr. Jeremy Fry and his wife and family at their home near Bath. It was Mr. Fry who, four months later, was announced as the official best man at the Westminster Abbey ceremony at which Tony and Margaret were to be married.

He was a long-time friend of Armstrong-Jones and they had known each other before Mr. Fry married. Possibly it was during this weekend that the question of marriage and all the plans attendant to it were first mentioned by the happy couple.

However, as all the world knows, Mr. Fry had to cancel his acceptance of the best man duty at the last moment. It was officially announced that he had a recurrence of jaundice, an illness which had attacked him some years earlier. It caused a sensation almost as great as the original engagement announcement.

During those last few weeks leading up to Christmas 1959, Tony was rarely able to keep out of Clarence House, it seemed. Hardly a day passed without his appearance there and most evenings he and Margaret spent huddled together in the sitting room, perhaps on one of the settees, talking animatedly together.

Or, more often than not, I suspect, he would tease her into thinking they would sit at home and then lead her off on some gay nighttime exploit which he had arranged to surprise her.

It was during these last few happy weeks of my service at Clarence House more than at any other time in that truly memorable year that I saw the real beauty of my Princess and realized the full significance of the saying: "A woman in love is a thing of beauty."

She became, in the eyes of all who saw her at close hand, the living image of the spirit of happiness. And in my role as "Cupid's Aide" I made sure that the young couple were never disturbed during the long hours they were alone together at the House and at Windsor Royal Lodge.

No longer was Margaret acting like a Royal Princess. She was simply a gay, excited young woman who was giving her whole soul to the job of being in love.

Their romance had taken root and blossomed forth within a mile of Buckingham Palace, yet even at that late date, I felt certain that the secret I held for them was not shared even by Margaret's sister, the Queen.

Maybe this accounted for some of the resentment—that seems to me to be only word to use—that appeared to mark the Queen's attitude right up to the time she sat in the Abbey and watched the ceremony going on before her.

But even if the Queen did not share my opinion, and despite some of the sneers I have heard in high places since, I regarded the Margaret-Tony affair as a fairy-tale romance in the best Ruritanian musical-comedy style.

I had seen it through a summer so beautiful it might have been fashioned by the Gods especially for their benefit. Now it was continuing into December, and Christmas and a New Year were days away. But the love between Margaret and Tony was as warm as the climate was growing cold.

Chapter Sixteen

This is the final chapter in my story, for it ends the week before Christmas.

I had seen Margaret and the Queen Mother leave the house for the journey to Norfolk where, as always, they were to spend their Christmas with the rest of the Family.

I can still vividly remember the last time I helped Margaret into her car. It was the last time I was to touch her or see her close-up. She was wrapped in a big fur coat and was carrying one or two parcels in her arms. I settled her in the back seat, arranged a rug over her knees and stepped back to close the car door.

Then Margaret leaned forward with a gentle smile and spoke her last words to me.

"A merry Christmas to you, John," she said simply.

And I replied: "A very merry Christmas to you, Your Royal Highness ... and a happy New Year."

I slammed the door and she lifted her hand a little in a kind of salute-cum-wave and off she drove. My life with Princess Margaret was at an end.

It was unfortunate for me, but the decision had already formed in my mind that I would have to leave Clarence House. I had wrestled with the problem for weeks, but even my shaky mathematics had made it quite plain that even the honor of serving my Princess could not compensate for my poor wages.

Had all things been equal, I think I would have been perfectly content to carry on. Finances apart, I loved the life. I was truly devoted to my Princess and would have gone to the ends of the earth for her.

But I had personal commitments which made it harder

and harder to resist the lure of more highly-paid jobs which my service at Clarence House had opened up for me.

With a heavy heart, I resigned.

My last day at Clarence House was the day after New Year's Day.

On that chilly morning, I stood alone in my little room— the room that I had so disliked when first I arrived—and surveyed my meager possessions. I had packed them all in the same suitcase that I had brought with me to Clarence House. Now I snapped it shut and carried it to the top of the stairs.

I went back into the room and picked up, from the top of it was jolted by the smash of rifle butts as the ceremonial the chest of drawers, the two things I treasure most in the world—the exquisite leather-bound lighter and cigarette case which had been my Christmas present from my Princess. She had picked them out herself and had had the initial "M" engraved in gold on the corner of both.

Quite alone—for I had said my goodbys to the few staff members who still remained at the house over the holiday— I trudged across the courtyard to the main gate. I paused here and took a last long look at Clarence House.

Then I turned on my heels and with a nod to the policeman on duty there, strode out of the gate.

It crashed shut behind me, and I knew then that a little piece of me had been locked in there behind me.

I thought of the finality of that sound as I stood in the crowds outside the Abbey five months later. My memory of guard crashed to the alert for the reappearance of my Princess—now the wife of Antony Armstrong-Jones.

They walked from the Abbey, while the world around me went mad with joy. Margaret, her hand laid gently on Tony's arm, glowed with the fire of inner happiness. Even at this distance, she looked absolutely adorable.

She climbed slowly into her coach, trailing yards and yards of wedding train behind her. Tony climbed in and the snorting horses strained and eased the ornate carriage into motion.

It circled and, through the maze of waving flags, cameras and little children held aloft, I caught my last distant glimpse of the Princess, beautiful, content and—did I imagine it?—very slightly triumphant.

"Isn't she the loveliest thing you ever saw?" asked a woman standing next to me.

"I wonder what she's really like?"

I said nothing, but turned to move with the slowly melting crowd.

"If only you knew," I thought. "If only you knew . . . ."